RELATIONSHIP COMMUNICATION FOR COUPLE

BY

AARON SCOTT

HOW TO DEAL WITH DISCUSSION IN MAINTAINING REAL RESPECT AND LOVE & HOW TO IMPROVE YOUR COMMUNICATION SKILLS

Table of Contents

INTRODUCTION

Relationship Communication is very important in sustaining a marriage. Communication problems in relationship are often the primary issue of failed marriages. So, to make sure that your marriage doesn't fail because of communication, you need to learn to develop good communication skills in your relationship. Here are 7 tips to get better at it.

Have you always been able to explain your message clearly? Sometimes, when couples are communicating, they tend to expect the other party to understand what they say even when they only leave the sentence half finished. For example, you say, "Darling, can you help me to buy toilet rolls back..?" Your spouse bought back the toilet rolls, but it is not the usual brand you want. Communication like this can get couples to argue so just make sure you get your message across properly by saying it more detail.

Ask if you do not understand. Sometimes, the "don't bother" attitude can cause your communication and relationship to suffer. I often hear couples complaining about their partners do not care about them a lot. The fact is sometimes because of laziness or the take for granted attitude will cause frictions between couples.

Don't expect your partner to be a mind reader all the time. Some people choose to keep quiet and let their spouses guess what their needs and thinking are. If you have specific needs, you need to communicate out to your partner. Keeping inside your heart is no good for the relationship. If you want your partner to be more romantic, just say it!

Be transparent in your conversation. Nobody will like their own wife or husband to hide any big secrets from them. You need to be truthful not only to yourself, but also your spouse.

"I am too tired to hear anything today, let's talk tomorrow." When both of you first started dating, there always seem to be endless topic to chat throughout the whole night. Of course, I do not expect both of you to behave same as the initial stage of dating, but putting in effort to have meaningful chat together everyday can help to improve the relationship.

Have the basic respect to listen to your spouse when he or she is talking. It is better not to have that kind of thinking like "Hey, you should listen to me, whatever things I say, I am always right." Always right? Isn't that too chauvinistic?

No patience towards the spouse is also a common problem in a relationship. You still need patience for many things in your relationship. You need to have the patience to listen, patience to speak and patience to do things for your partner. Often, we get a lot easier to show out our emotions to someone we know very well. Well, if it gets too much, you will start to see problems appearing in your relationship soon.

COMMUNICATION BETWEEN COUPLES

Good communication is an important part of all relationships and is an essential part of any healthy partnership. All relationships have ups and downs, but a healthy communication style can make it easier to deal with conflict, and build a stronger and healthier partnership. We often hear how important communication is, but not what it is and how we can use good communication in our relationships.

By definition, communication is the transfer of information from one place to another. In relationships, communication allows to you explain to someone else what you are experiencing and what your needs are. The act of communicating not only helps to meet your needs, but it also helps you to be connected in your relationship.

Communicating clearly in a relationship

Talk to each other. No matter how well you know and love each other, you cannot read your partner's mind. We need to communicate clearly to avoid misunderstandings that may cause hurt, anger, resentment or confusion.

It takes two people to have a relationship and each person has different communication needs and styles. Couples need to find a way of communicating that suits their relationship. Healthy communication styles require practice and hard work; however communication will never be perfect all the time.

Be clear when communicating with your partner, so that your message can be received and understood. Double check your understanding of what your partner is saying.

When you talk to your partner, try to:

Set aside time to talk without interruption from other people or distractions like phones, computers or television

Think about what you want to say

Be clear about what you want to communicate

Make your message clear, so that your partner hears it accurately and understands what you mean

Talk about what is happening and how it affects you

Talk about what you want, need and feel – use 'I' statements such as 'I need', 'I want' and 'I feel'

Accept responsibility for your own feelings

Listen to your partner. Put aside your own thoughts for the time being and try to understand their intentions, feelings, needs and wants (this is called empathy)

Share positive feelings with your partner, such as what you appreciate and admire about them, and how important they are to you

Be aware of your tone of voice

Negotiate and remember that you don't have to be right all the time. If the issue you are having is not that important, sometimes let the issue go, or agree to disagree.

When we communicate, we can say a lot without speaking. Our body posture, tone of voice and the expressions on our face all convey a message. These non-verbal means of communicating can tell the other person how we feel about them.

If our feelings don't fit with our words, it is often the non-verbal communication that gets 'heard' and believed. For example, saying 'I love you' to your partner in a flat, bored, tone of voice, gives two very different messages. Notice whether your body language reflects what you are saying.

Listening and communication

Listening is a very important part of effective communication. A good listener can encourage their partner to talk openly and honestly. Tips for good listening include:

Keep comfortable eye contact (where culturally appropriate)

Lean towards the other person and make gestures to show interest and concern

Have an open, non-defensive, fairly relaxed posture with your arms and legs uncrossed

Face the other person – don't sit or stand sideways

Sit or stand on the same level to avoid looking up to or down on the other person

Avoid distracting gestures such as fidgeting with a pen, glancing at papers, or tapping your feet or fingers

Be aware that physical barriers, noise or interruptions will make good communication difficult. Mute telephones or other communication devices to ensure you are really listening

Let the other person speak without interruption

Show genuine attention and interest

Use assertive statements like 'I feel …. About …', 'What I need is…'

Be aware of your tone

Be prepared to take time out if you are feeling really angry about something. It might be better to calm down before you address the issue

Ask for feedback from the other person on your listening.

Open and clear communication can be learnt. Some people find it hard to talk and may need time and encouragement to express their views. These people may be good listeners, or they may be people whose actions speak louder than their words.

You can help to improve your communication by:

Building companionship – sharing experiences, interests and concerns with your partner, and showing affection and appreciation

Sharing intimacy – intimacy is not only a sexual connection. Intimacy is created by having moments of feeling close and attached to your partner. It means being able to comfort and be comforted, and to be open and honest. An act of intimacy can be as simple as bringing your partner a cup of tea because you can tell they are tired

Being on the same page as your partner. It's important that you and your partner are both in agreement on key issues in your relationship, such as how finances are distributed, what key goals you have and you're parenting styles.

To improve the way you communicate, start by asking questions such as:

What things cause conflict between you and your partner? Are they because you are not listening to each other?

What things bring you happiness and feelings of connection?

What things cause you disappointment and pain?

What things don't you talk about and what stops you talking about them?

How would you like your communication with your partner to be different?

If possible, ask these questions with your partner and share your responses. Consider, and try, ways to communicate differently. See whether the results improve your communication. When you are more aware of how you communicate, you will be able to have more control over what happens between you. While it may not be easy at first, opening up new areas of communication can lead to a more fulfilling relationship.

Some things are difficult to communicate

Most of us find some experiences or topics difficult to talk about. It may be something that is painful or makes us feel uncomfortable. For example, some people find it difficult to express their emotions. It is often the things that cannot be talked about that hurt the most.

If you are having difficulty expressing yourself, or talking with your partner about something, you might find it helps to talk to a counselor.

Managing conflict with communication

Avoid using the silent treatment.

Don't jump to conclusions. Find out all the facts rather than guessing at motives.

Discuss what actually happened. Don't judge.

Learn to understand each other, not to defeat each other.

Talk using the future and present tense, not the past tense.

Concentrate on the major problem, and don't get distracted by other minor problems.

Talk about the problems that hurt your or your partner's feelings, and then move on to problems about differences in opinions.

Use 'I feel' statements, not 'You are' statements.

Back to top

Seeking help for communication issues

If you can't seem to improve the communication in your relationship, consider talking with a relationship counselor. Counselors are trained to recognize the patterns in a couple's communication that are causing problems and to help change those patterns.

You could also consider doing a course that is relevant to your relationship. It is better to act early and talk to someone about your concerns, rather than wait until things get worse.

IMPORTANCE OF COMMUNICATION BETWEEN COUPLES

Communication is rightly defined as the transfer of information from one person to another. There are many ways of communicating with people around us, such as; speaking personally, using the phone and writing letters. Since man is a social animal, communication is his need. It is almost impossible for a person to survive without socializing or communicating with others.

This factor also applies to two people who are in a relation with each other. Even though marriage is known to be the sole phase of responsibility, two persons are equally responsible for each other's lives in many ways. And when there is no communication between the two, there can be problems like; insecurities, loss of faith, emotional dissatisfaction leading to the loss of interest in the relationship.

Relationships are not difficult to maintain, if they involve healthy communication among one other. When each one knows how the other person thinks and feels about certain things, there is more openness and freedom in the relation, thus making it easier to maintain it. Communication is the only means by which you can know about the person you are interested in and when you know the way he/she is, maintaining a relationship with him or her becomes easy.

The importance of communication in marriage is often not taken seriously as many couples tend to think that the daily banter or the lack of it doesn't affect them on a day-to-day basis. But communication is the vehicle through which all other important parts of marriage are performed. If you love someone, but you don't use your words and your actions to communicate it, you're not doing right by your partner. If you trust someone, let them know. Communicate it to them. If you can communicate honestly, your marriage has a good chance of being happy and healthy. In fact, the importance of communication should be considered right from the courtship days as it sets the right foundation of the relationship.

Open husband and wife communication is the cornerstone of any and every long and loving marriage. The problem is that some people just aren't good at it. Let's take some time to understand the importance of communication in marriage and see what forms of marital communication will create the atmosphere of a strong and caring marriage.

Communication as a cornerstone

Love, trust, honesty, and every other important characteristic of a strong marriage aren't meaningful in themselves. It is the expression of these things that produces a marriage worth envying. Showing that love, showcasing your trust, and acting honestly is where the magic is. Being able to communicate how much your wife or husband means to you is where your marriage goes from good to great.

Communication is more than just speaking, though. There is verbal communication, nonverbal communication, and physical acts that can be placed under the umbrella of communication.

Communication Keeps a Couple Closer than they think

How can someone know another individual for who they really are? We don't get premonitions or have the power to read other people's minds. By sharing our life's stories and incidents, we can be sure to intimately involve ourselves with someone. Same goes in a marriage. More than just having physical contact, the emotional connection is also important. When we have shared small instances from our lives, no matter what it is (something like wanting to bake cookies at home, going out for a long drive, wishing to paint the walls together), any kind of openness will bring a couple together and make them feel as one. When you know what is going on in your spouse's mind and heart, you can resolve issues more quickly and effectively.

Assumptions and Misunderstandings won't Creep In

It is a natural that when your spouse isn't sharing particular information with you, our mind tends to wander off and think of the worse. When a couple talks to one another without any inhibitions, they eliminate the negativeness out of their lives and keep misunderstandings at bay. After knowing each others' likes, dislikes, opinions, beliefs, wants, and desires in life, you two made the decision to see this marriage through. So what is stopping you now? Opening your heart to someone you love should be looked upon as a blessing because you know that there is at least one person in your life who accepts you for who you are. Keeping a verbal gap between you two will only bring in disappointment and insecurity.

Lack of Communication can Lead Towards Infidelity

Let's look at our question on communication from a different angle. What does not communicating with someone lead to? When your spouse doesn't share things with you, he/she isn't sharing his/her life. Keeping things to yourself, avoiding any major conversations or arguments, wanting to be alone rather than spend time together, all these factors play a major role in separating a couple and breaking their bond. This may not be the case with all the couples, but sometimes, not being emotionally connected with your spouse might give you ideas of making this connection with someone else. No matter how much a person can try to stop themselves from taking this path, when the heart isn't fulfilled with its own needs, it tries to satisfy it elsewhere.

Good Communication Means you Respect your Spouse Enough to be Honest

Many a time, when we don't wish to talk to our spouse, we tend to make up some stories and end the conversation right then and there. This may work in your favor once or twice, but over the course of time, you might just want to get out of any situation with making up lies. When there is nothing to hide from your spouse, what is the need to bring in false information and ruin your chances of having a beautiful life with someone. Initially, it may seem innocent to keep certain things from your spouse, but this behavior only highlights the fact that you don't respect your spouse and be honest with him/her. You owe it to him/her to let in on what is going in your life, your mind, and how can you both handle the situations and move forward.

Communication is a Two-way Street with No Red Lights

Talking to someone doesn't end at you sharing what was on your mind (anger, frustration, news) and go your separate ways. To communicate means being there for one another whenever your spouse needs you and emotionally comforting him/her. Often times, couples feel that sharing means saying what they want and leaving the room. In fact, when you open yourself to your spouse, you also open the possibility of receiving information as well. In a marriage, or life in general, we all look towards being needed, wanted by someone. And when a couple, who is married, is there for each other, no problems are tough enough, no arguments are important enough to break them apart.

REASONS FOR COMMUNICATION BETWEEN COUPLES

Saves You Money

There's no doubt about it, poor communications can be costly. Flowers, candy, gifts large and small are regularly offered by a spouse who said the "wrong thing' or failed to say the "right thing." When you look at costly mistakes in a marriage the majority of them are a result of poor communications.

Saves Time

"Yeah" "Sure" "Whatever" may seem like an efficient way of dealing with your husband or wife when they want to talk but it's not. Sooner or later an unresolved issue must be discussed. So taking the time the first time your spouse wants to talk with you will ultimately prove to be a time saver. You won't have to go back to the beginning and start again, because you communicated clearly and honestly the first time around.

Earns Points For The Future

Every time you and your spouse have a satisfying conversation you build credit toward future communication. Both of you know and expect that you will be able to share because you have a record of success.

It's Good For Your Health

Good communications in marriage reduces stress for two reasons. First, it allows you to resolve the tension between you, and second, it allows you to "vent' some of your anxieties from other areas of your life. Many couples report that their partner is the first person they could fully trust. "I can tell him anything", one wife said recently. "I know he will listen and understand how I feel."

Allows You To Concentrate On Other Things

Have you ever found yourself continuing a discussion you had earlier while you were at work? "I should have said this" you say to yourself. "Oh yeah? Well what about the time you did..." Perhaps you're so upset about an unfinished conversation earlier in the day that you call your spouse to either apologize or get one more point across. Listening and talking effectively resolves the issue and frees your mind to concentrate on other tasks.

Builds Up Your Relationship

Couples who don't communicate are in danger of losing love and affection for one another. All relationships are nourished by communications. If you don't communicate with parents, siblings, co-workers, children, or your partner, you lose touch with them and your relationship withers.

You Learn More About Yourself

Have you ever tried to explain your thoughts or feelings to someone else and during the conversation you end up in a different place from where you began? Putting your thoughts into words forces you to clarify them. Talking and listening also allows you to fine tune your ideas.

Less Hassle

"Why won't you talk to me?" "I know something is bothering you-what is it?" "Don't just walk away. Talk to me. Please!"

Be honest. Avoiding communications is as much work as communicating. So why not just talk, or do you like being pursued? Does being silent give you more control over the situation? While it may seem that way, ultimately you'll have a spouse who will trust you less. Giving your partner the gift of your time to talk things through will make your life simpler in the long run.

You Might Learn Something New

The person you are married to is not the person you first met. Neither are you the same. Every day brings new experiences, thoughts, dreams, plans. It's a guarantee that if you work at communicating you will discover new things about each other.

These new discoveries stretch out in two directions from where you are now. You will discover experiences from your spouse's childhood that you never knew. You don't know them because the person you love has them hidden away in their memory. They don't remember until some new experience triggers a recollection.

You see a child run into the street and your husband says, "I almost got hit by a car when I was that age." What follows is a story of childhood excitement, parental fear, and lessons learned that come pouring out from the distant past. It might explain why he drives so slowly in areas with children, or give you insight into how he will react when your child does the same thing years from now.

COMMUNICATION RULES FOR A GREAT RELATIONSHIP

Communication is a challenge for anyone, even at the best of times. But why is communication so difficult, especially in relationships?

While part of it stems from a relatively universal fear of letting others get close, each of us brings our own hang-ups to the table. Sometimes, we aren't even aware of them. No wonder communicating someone else — who has his or her own hang-ups — is so hard!

In order to minimize the risk of miscommunication, it's essential to take charge of the challenge. There are certain steps anyone can take to try and ensure that our messages are properly received and interpreted by our partners (and all others, really).

1. Don't make assumptions about your partner's feelings.

People quite often assume that their partner automatically "knows" what they are thinking/feeling/knowing. Does this sound familiar to you? Or have you ever thought to yourself, "If my partner truly loved me, he/she would (fill in the blank here) _____"?

In order to receive the kind of love that you need in a relationship, it's best to share with your partner what your "language of love" is by verbally communicating it. People aren't mind-readers after all.

To do this, you first need to get in touch with what your own needs and desires are — and for some that can be the hardest part. Perhaps you feel most loved by being cuddled and hugged frequently. Or, maybe it's having your partner do things around the house for you.

Remember, too, that sometimes it takes more than one telling to get the message across. Don't automatically assume that your partner knows how to demonstrate to you his/her love, because they may have a different interpretation of what a loving relationship entails than you do!

2. Ask questions to find out what your partner believes about love.

What your partner understands about loving you, and perhaps also what they don't know, enables you to equip them with the tools and awareness that they need in order to be able to support you in the way that you need to be loved. Don't keep repeating the criticism, "He should have known ..." or "I've told her 100 times that ..." Repetition tends to be a necessary component in communication. (And with that, so is patience!)

3. Be honest about when you're the one causing problems.

Do you find yourself evaluating your partner's behavior, and often taking things personally because "they just don't get it"? Is it possible that you haven't clearly articulated your needs sufficiently in order to experience that they got the message? Or maybe it is time to go to the spa so you can work on developing a little patience.

Perhaps you need to stop expecting, in order to help remove some of the roadblocks in the way, so that they can deliver the love you are seeking.

4. Get clarity on your partner's perspective.

As we enter into a relationship, we often forget which perspective we are looking from — typically our own! However, our partner also has his/her own perspective. This can lead to different interpretations, and different expectations. It's necessary to talk about perspectives, and work out any differences.

Also, this may need to be done over and over, throughout the evolution and progression of the relationship. As people grow and change, so do their expectations and perceptions. This alone can have a profound impact on a relationship.

5. Realize that you're always giving AND always receiving in a relationship.

If you always assume that no matter how much you give, you're equally receiving that much and more; you'll never have an empty bucket.

In other words: in order to give, you first have to receive. There are myriad ways you may be receiving — from Spirit, from God, from church, from self-love, from awesome experiences, from knowledge. Perhaps it's not the fact that you're not receiving, but that your "receiving receptor" has the volume turned down, and you're not taking your gifts into account.

Once this has been brought to your awareness, how do you turn this receiving receptor volume up so that you recognize the place(s) from which you receive? Once you can identify this pattern (or whatever your individual patterns are), you will have greater access to the love you have to give.

Inside of a healthy relationship, people fundamentally have love already. There need not be an uncertainty about whether it exists. It's "ever-present." What commonly interferes with our ability to give or receive our partner's love are our own interactions and our internal criticism.

So get radically honest with yourself, and identify the elements of your inner dialogue that could be kinder and more gentle. The time is now to cultivate love for yourself.

COMMUNICATION BETWEEN COUPLES: HOW TO COMMUNICATE IN A RELATIONSHIP

Most people have never learned how to communicate. Without this skill, a person is handicapped in an intimate relationship. Without being able to express themselves and listen to another, partners cannot achieve intimacy. By developing your communication skills, you and your partner will be able to establish and preserve a loving, respectful relationship between two people who love each other.

The Purpose of Communication in Relationships

One of the biggest problems in communicating is that most couples have a basic misconception of what the purpose of communication is. Most approach talking with a partner as a debate in which each presents a preconceived version of the reality of what is going on between the two partners.

The fault with this approach is the mistaken assumption that either partner can go into the conversation with an accurate perception of reality. This is not possible because neither person has the necessary information to determine what reality is, that is: what is going on between them.

One purpose of communication is to determine what reality is. Communication involves the collaboration of two people as they share and examine all of their perceptions, feelings, ideas and thoughts to come to an accurate understanding of what is happening.

Collaborative Communication

Everyone knows that communication is simply a matter of talking and listening. However, most of us mistakenly believe that the matter of communicating is simple. We fail to realize that rather than involving innate abilities, communication involves specific skills can be learned and developed in ourselves in order to talk with and listen to our loved ones.

Step 1: Approaching a Conversation with Your Relationship Partner

Rule #1 to follow when going into a conversation with your partner: unilaterally disarm. That is, give up the need to be right!! You are not going into a battle that you have to win.

This is not to say that you are will have to compromise or capitulate. This is not to say that you can't be angry, frustrated or provoked. You have a right to all of your thoughts and feelings.

Just consider that your partner may have something to say that is worth listening to and considering. This conversation is not a battleground where you must prove that you are right; it is not a fight that you must win.

Step 2: Talking to Your Relationship Partner

Going into a conversation, there is only one reality that a person can be sure of: you can know what your own thoughts, feelings and perceptions are. You can be sure of nothing else: not the other person's thoughts, feelings or perceptions; not even the reality of what is going on between the two of you.

The only thing that you and your partner each needs to bring to the conversation is something that each of you can be sure of: your own thoughts, feelings and perceptions.   However, talking personally about yourself is often more challenging than you might think.

Focus on yourself.

It is an unfortunate reality that, within almost all couples, one person is victimized by the other. As a result, the focus of many of their discussions is on blaming each other. In your effort to talk about yourself, avoid the temptation to lapse into attacking, accusing, criticizing or blaming your partner.

You are here to talk about you. Not about your partner or the kids or work or your friends. About you. What would you say about yourself? Look at your partner and think of what you could reveal about yourself to him-her at this moment.

Reveal feelings that are embarrassing or humiliating.

It is important to recognize your irrational feelings. Don't dismiss them as being inappropriate, immature or meaningless. Make an effort to talk about the feelings that you would much rather skip over. The feelings that you fear will cause you embarrassment or humiliation should you disclose them.

For example, if you feel hurt or disappointed discuss these feelings with your partner. Avoid the temptation to defend yourself by becoming victimized and righteous. This is not about how you shouldn't be hurt or disappointed. It is just about the simple truth that you are hurt or disappointed, and that it is causing you emotional pain.

Reveal your personal wants.

People often feel embarrassed to talk about what they want. Not the easy wants: I want to go to that new restaurant, I want a new jacket, and I want to go on a trip. But the personal wants that come from deep down in you where you feel the most vulnerable: I want you to complement me, I want to be affectionate with you, and I want to have a baby with you.

Many of us have grown up feeling ashamed of our wants. However, the more that you communicate on this level, the more in touch with yourself you will be—the more authentic you will be as a person—the closer your partner will be able to feel to you.

When you and your partner communicate on this personal level, many of the trivial issues between you vanish. It becomes apparent that they were merely inconsequential issues meant to distract you in your relationship.

Finally, talk to your partner with the decency and respect with which you talk to anyone else.

Most people have a special way of communicating that they reserve for their partners. What makes it special is that it includes abusive behaviors such as:

being complaining, demanding, bossy, irritable, sarcastic, childish, parental, and condescending...to name a few.

When you are talking with your partner, stop and ask yourself: "Would I be talking like this to anyone else?" Do you hear yourself complaining (I'm so tired!) or demanding (Get me a drink of water!!) or deferring (What should I order for dinner?) in ways you never hear yourself with other people?

Try to treat your partner with the respect and decency with which you treat any other person....after all, your partner is another person.

Step 3: Listening to Your Relationship Partner

Going into a conversation, you have very little awareness of what your partner really thinks and feels. You may think you do because you recognize an expression that he-she always gets when he-she is hurt. Or you might have even exchanged some heated words. But until you have listened to your partner, you know almost nothing.

Listening is a skill that needs to be learned and developed. Just because we hear does not mean that we are listening. Only when we listen with an unconditional interest in understanding the person who is talking to us, can we truly get to know that person.

Listening is not about you.

Listening is entirely about the person you are listening to. Put aside your point of view. Your thoughts, opinions or reactions to what the other person is saying are both irrelevant and inappropriate. The person talking is not looking to you for advice or guidance. What they truly need is to be heard so that they feel that they are being seen.

Hear your partner out.
When you put yourself aside, that is when you focus on what your partner is saying rather than on how you are reacting, you are making yourself available to listen to your partner. As your partner talks, try to sense what it feels like to be him-her.

Try to feel what your partner is experiencing. Empathize. Listen with your heart. When he-she relates an incident to you, try to feel how he-she felt in the situation. Make a special effort to empathize with what your partner is currently feeling while talking with you.

Indicate that you are hearing your partner.

It is not enough to listen silently. It is helpful to indicate to your partner that you are hearing him-her. During your conversation, reflect what your partner is saying and feeling.

If your reflection is not accurate, your partner can correct you. You can then make adjustments until you have a true understanding of what your partner is trying to communicate to you. Reflecting lets your partner know that he-she is being heard, which makes him-her feeling seen by you.

Have compassion for your partner.

As you listen to your partner with empathy and feel what he-she feels, you gain compassion for him-her as a person. You feel for him-her as a human being with personal pain and struggles like the rest of us.

You gain a new perspective. When you feel for your partner's issues, your own personal over-reactions to them seem unimportant. Giving advice or being judgmental suddenly seems condescending and patronizing. Acting hurt or victimized suddenly seems childish and self-indulgent. From this perspective, you see your partner as a separate person who you care about deeply as he-she deals with his-her own issues in life.

Step 4: Determine Reality with Your Relationship Partner

In the process of talking personally about yourself as your partner truly listened, it is likely that you both came to a deeper understanding of what you were experiencing and feeling. Likewise, as your partner talked personally to you with you truly listening, both of you most likely came to a deeper understanding of your partner's experiences and feelings.

This level of insight and understanding along with the feelings of empathy and compassion that accompany it, help clarify much of the confusion that exists within the couple. The deeper awareness of each other eliminates many of the misconceptions, misinterpretations and miscommunications that go into creating this confusion. What remains is a clearer picture of yourselves and of the reality of your relationship.

At this point in the conversation, you and your partner may want to review what you have learned about yourselves and each other and about your relationship. By discussing what you have learned, you can identify the personal issues and reactions that tend to lead to trouble between you. You will now know what to look out for to avoid trouble in the future. And if you do get into trouble with each other, you can recognize what is happening and deal with it more quickly.

Helpful Advice about Communication

There are several negative forms of communication to be aware of. Make sure that you are not engaging in any of these because they contaminate the communication process. As long as you are enlisting these techniques, you can be sure that you and your partner will become more and more alienated and estranged from each other.

Communication should bring you and your partner closer to each other. It should be used to break down the barriers that keep you apart, not to build up fortifications between you.

Intimidation: A Common Relationship Issue

One of the most effective techniques that couples use to manipulate, control and punish each other is intimidation. According to the dictionary, to intimidate is to frighten into submission.

Interestingly enough, couples report that the behaviors they are intimidated by are not those that are overt and aggressive. Rather partners are frightened by the subtle covert behaviors that leave them feeling guilty and responsible for their mate's unhappiness.

During a conversation between a couple, if one partner responds by being miserable, self-hating or self-destructive, it is virtually impossible for the other partner not to submit. The conversation is over; the intimidating partner has won.

But in reality, both people have suffered disastrous defeats. The dictionary goes on to say that to intimidate "implies reduction to a state where the spirit is broken or all courage is lost." This certainly defines the emotional state of the partner who has been frightened into submission. Likewise, the cost to intimidating person is also high. The intimidating partner must forfeit his-her autonomy, after which his-her spirit is broken and courage is lost.

Parental or Childish Communicating

Watch out for ways that you might be communicating from a childish or parental stance. Childish communications involve deferring and submitting, looking for direction or definition, being servile or subservient, seeking approval and/or criticism. Parental communications involve directing and dominating, being condescending and assertive, acting judgmental and critical.

None of these qualities has a place in the communications between two independent adults in an equal relationship. Be respectful of yourself and respectful of your partner in the way that you speak to each other.

Non-verbal Communication in Relationships

Non-verbal communication refers to how one's body language contributes to the process of communicating feelings and reactions. Non-verbal communication is not a negative form of communicating. On the contrary, it can be very helpful in trying to understand what a person is saying.

Sometimes what a person is saying does not coincide with what he-she is communicating non-verbally. These mixed messages often cause confusion. First you must acknowledge both messages, even though they conflict. Then you have to decide which one more accurately communicates what the person is thinking or feeling. Often the non-verbal message is more truthful.

Many of these mixed messages are communicated in couple relationships. A partner may say "I love you" throughout the day then behave indifferently and unaffectionately. A partner may declare interest and concern about his/her mate but whenever the mate talks about him-herself, the partner actually interrupts or becomes distracted.

Pay attention to what your actions are saying. Make your actions and words match. In other words, be truthful in how you communicate both verbally and non-verbally.

EFFECTIVE COMMUNICATION TECHNIQUES FOR COUPLES

Good communication skills are the keys to any successful relationship because relationships are emotional and rely on interpersonal verbal and nonverbal exchanges between the two people involved. Most marriages start out with the idea of success not realizing the number one cause of divorce is bad communication. In cases of parenting and co-parenting, communication is even more important because the parents are raising children who will become adults. Kids learn their first communication techniques from their parents or guardians. There are three types of communications: verbal, nonverbal, and written. Below are the top 10 effective communication techniques for couples. This list was derived from Meta research of many lists from the internet, books, interviews and this author's past experience.

1. Do not talk at the same time – listen!

This may seem obvious but when emotions are running high, each person wants to get their point across and a subliminal power struggle comes into play signifying that no one is really interested in the conversation or resolution. Please do not interrupt each other. Constant interruption is stating you do not think the other person has anything important to say and that you just want your way. The reason for the conversation is to hear each other's point of view. Resist the urge to interrupt.

2. Think before you speak or you will regret it

"Give me the gift of a listening heart." – said King Solomon. You may say something that can't be taken back, ever. If talking in person is just impossible, try written communication but please stay off the internet. You are communicating personal feelings to each other. Text each other in short sentences. Write a letter or note. However, real time communication is better. NO CAPS please. Typing in all caps gives the impression you are shouting. I LOVE YOU is permitted. Remember, you do love each other.

3. Give a hoot – care

When communicating with your spouse or partner, it is so important to not lose sight that the communication is to make the relationship bond tighter not break up. Put yourself in the other person's shoes. Try to understand why they may feel the way they do. Do they have all the facts? Do they just want attention from you? Regardless, treat their feelings as if they are important.

For example, if your partner expresses concern about not getting invited to a social event that was important to them. You on the other hand think the whole thing is silly. Restrain from expressing your thoughts and empathize with your partner. "I know this was important to you but let's try to find out why we were not invited so that we can get invited to the next event or one similar." It may never happen but your partner will love you for that. It's the little things that count.

4. No hitting below the belt

Please watch your language. One of the things that will terminate effective communication is name calling or bringing up something that happened a long time ago. Especially, a situation that was resolved or forgiven. Please try to avoid the words "you" and "you always." These words will surely take your conversation in a negative direction. Try calling your partner's first name lovingly instead. This technique dilutes anger. It changes the tone of the conversation.

5. Facts please

A general rule among long time married couples is, you can ask about it but if you can't prove it then you have to let it go. In other words, if there is no proof, don't bring it to the table. Suspicion is one thing but to accuse someone of it is another matter. Many partners get tired of being accused of cheating. Many cheaters claim that they were accused of cheating all the time, so they decided to actually do it. It's normal to be a little jealous when it comes to the love of your life but it is not normal to express it every time you feel it. Investigating discreetly is permitted but not accusing without being sure.

6. Participate with sincerity and honesty

A conversation is between two people. Silent treatment is not permitted. The opposite of love is not hate but indifference. When your partner is talking to you, talk back without any hidden motives. Communicate with transparency and honesty. Ask questions for clarity. If you are busy, ask for a time when it is better for the both of you. Do not just walk out the door or listen and not respond. Remember you are in this relationship together.

7. Observation

One way to communicate is to hear what your partner is not saying. Two people in a relationship get to learn each other fears, goals, values and dreams. No one should know your partner better than you, therefore, use that to your advantage and observe the situation. Some people are better at expressing themselves or communicating better than others. For example, Rita knew her husband, an advertising executive, wanted a new look. He had gained a few pounds so she thought he was self-conscious about it. She thought he wanted to be more attractive for her but after watching him look for clothes online, she realized he wanted a new look because he thought his style dated him and put him at a competitive disadvantage at work with his younger co-workers. It had nothing to do with their relationship. Rita hired a career stylist that solved her husband's problem.

8. Body language is a non-verbal communication technique

Even though body language is a thing to be observed, it speaks loudly. When your spouse is speaking, looking at him or her in the eyes means your partner has your undivided attention. Leaning forward, means you are interested in what they are saying; diverting eye contact is an indication of dishonesty. Learn your partner's body language. For example, Michael learned that Lisa had different walks for each of her moods. There was a walk when she was busy, there was one when she was angry, and a totally different walk when she was relaxed. Michael is often tuned into her body language to detect her mood and to pick a good time to talk to her. When communicating with your partner do not ignore their body language because that is how you can determine if they are understanding you, agreeing, or disagreeing.

9. Respect – agree to disagree

Never lose sight of the fact that you two are on the same team and there is no reason to degrade each other or fight because there will always be another issue down the road. Couples who learn to solve problems together are the most successful. Every problem will not be solvable because you and your partner are individuals who will have different opinions from time to time. Realize the relationship is bigger than any problem. In addition, respect your partner by being a confidant who can be depended upon. Sherry and her husband Mike of ten years never agree on political candidates. It was a bit like sports and they were rooting for opposing teams. However, at the end of an election, they were always on the same team regardless of political issues.

10. Witnesses or third party intervention

Many couples seek counseling, a trusted friend or a family member to play a neutral party in an important decision. This is not a bad idea. A third person may bring a different perspective to the situation. Just be sure the person is a confidant and has the qualifications to help you with the problem. For example, Janet wanted her husband to be a little less traditional. He was very old-fashioned in his ideas of women's roles in marriage. He never washed a dish or did any housework. Janet worked. She and Bob just had a new baby. Janet felt she needed more help from Bob. He did not agree. Janet went to Bob's father for assistance. He talked with Bob and shared his own experiences of shifting his views of the role of a man in the family. Afterward, Bob started helping out.

In conclusion, effective communication is one of the top skills couples can learn to improve their relationship or marriage. These interpersonal communication skills are verbal, nonverbal, and written communication. Among the top 10 effective communication techniques for couples are listening, fighting fair, getting the facts, caring, honesty, respecting, observing, obtaining third party interventions and active participation.

TYPES OF COMMUNICATION THAT DETERMINE YOUR RELATIONSHIPS

Communication, in the simplest form, is sending out a message and receiving it. Messages sent out take place in several different ways. Once you understand and learn to apply all 5 of these types of communication, you will be a master at getting and keeping solid personal and professional relationships.

1. Optical

Optical communication is "seeing" someone, having your sights set on someone, and noticing the existence of someone. The moment your peepers see another person and their peepers see you; the optical type of communication begins.

You see what they look like, what they are wearing, the hairdo, the facial expression, their body position, their body type, and instantly have thoughts like, "I like what I see," or "I will look elsewhere." If you like what you see and the other person likes what they see, then another decision as to "the next step" takes place. You or the other person will find a way to get closer and begin the second type of communication.

2. Auditory

Auditory communication is the most important of all types. This is the listening communication.

Wait, you mean to say that listening is communicating? I thought speaking is communicating?

Well, let me answer this question with asking you this: have you ever said something like "my dog just died," and the other person replied with "that's nice"? Why would anyone say it is nice that your dog died? Because they were not listening, they were not tuned in, and they were not interested. How did that make you feel? Do you think you would have gotten a better response had the person been "tuned in" and listened to what you said? You bet the response would have been more appropriate—this emphasizes the need for listening. When you are tuned in and listen to the other person, you are more likely to pick up on another type of communication: emotional.

3. Emotional

Emotional communication is so important to all aspects of beginning and moving forward in a relationship, so much so that Facebook finally caught up with the 5 additional reaction emojis to its "Like" button. These buttons allow a person to "react with emotion" to a post with more than just "like." They can now express love, laughter, anger, sadness, and amazement.

Why is it so important for Facebook to make this change to their "Like" button? For the same reason that I mentioned before with the example of the dog. The person in that example said "that's nice," and you were no doubt hurt that they reacted in a way that demonstrated inattentiveness and not listening. With these 5 emojis, people can react emotionally and more appropriately to messages that are posted. Now, when you post that your dog died, rather than receiving "likes," you'll get the "sad emoji," letting you know that others care.

Can you see that emotional communication really matters in a relationship? Whether it be a personal or professional relationship, an appropriate response will more likely keep that relationship moving forward.

4. Non-Verbal

Non-verbal communication includes tone of voice, pauses, rate of speech, facial expressions, body positions (i.e. crossed arms)—even walking away is a type of non-verbal communication. If you are speaking to someone and they smile, you will likely feel affirmed and that things are going well. If someone frowns in reaction to what you said, you get the message that someone disagrees with what you said. Non-verbal cues impact the understanding of what spoken and unspoken communication is taking place between people in a relationship.

5. Verbal

Verbal communication is using language in the form of sentences, phrases, and dialogue—but everyone already knows this, right?

In reality, it is much more than that. The words spoken can be misunderstood. However, there is a way to keep your words from being misunderstood.

Speak and watch for clues of acceptance. If you are really attentive, you can use words in your sentences, phrases, and dialogues that resonate more positively with the other person and will lead to a positive communication experience. A positive communication experience will lead to more positive experiences. This means more enjoyable interactions that will help to maintain the relationship and keep it moving forward.

By now, you have a more holistic approach to communicating in a relationship. Here is a hint: speak to the other person with expressions and be watchful for clues in the way the other person looks, listens, and reacts to you.

TOXIC COMMUNICATION

Couples communicate in different ways. However, often they communicate in ways that are destructive to their relationship rather than constructive. Below are the most common ways that couples communicate in destructive ways.

1. Trying to win

Perhaps the most usual type of bad communication is when couples are trying to win. The goal in this form of communication is not to resolve conflicts in a mutually respectful and accepting discussion of the issues. Instead one member of the couple (or both members) regard the discussion as a battle and therefore engage in tactics that are designed to win the battle.

Strategies used to win the battle include:

Guilt-tripping ("Oh, my God, I don't know how I put up with this!")

Intimidation ("Will you just shut up and listen to me for once?)

Constant complaining in order to wear the other person down ("How many times have I told you to empty the garbage?

Part of trying to win is about devaluing your spouse. You see your spouse as stubborn, hateful, selfish, egotistical, stupid or childish. Your goal in communication is to make your spouse see the light and submit to your superior knowledge and understanding. But in fact you never really win by using this kind of communication; you may make your spouse submit to a certain extent, but there will be a high price for that submission. There will be no real love in your relationship. It will be a loveless, dominant-submissive relationship.

2. Trying to be right

Another common kind of destructive communication comes out of the human tendency to want to be right. To some extent or another, we all want to be right. Hence, couples will often have the same argument over and over and nothing will ever be resolved.

"You're wrong!" one member will say. "You just don't get it!" The other member will say, "No, you're wrong. I'm the one who does everything and all you do is talk about how wrong I am." The first member will retort, "I talk about how wrong you are because you are wrong. And you just don't see it!"

Trying to be right

Couples who need to be right never get to the stage of being able to resolve conflicts because they can't give up their need to be right. In order to give up that need, one has to be willing and able to look at oneself objectively. Few can do that.

Confucius said, "I have traveled far and wide and have yet to meet a man who could bring the judgment to himself." The first step toward ending the right-wrong stalemate is to be willing to admit you may be wrong about something. Indeed you may be wrong about the things you are most adamant about.

3. Not communicating

Sometimes couples simply stop communicating. They hold everything inside and their feelings get acted out instead of expressed verbally. People stop communicating for various reasons:

They are afraid they won't be listened to;

They don't want to make themselves vulnerable;

Suppressing their anger because the other person isn't worthy of it;

They assume talking will lead to an argument. So each person lives independently and doesn't talk about anything to the other person that is important to them. They talk to their friends, but not to each other.

When couples stop communicating, their marriage becomes empty. They may go through the motions for years, maybe even until the very end. Their feelings, as I said, will be acted out in various ways. They are acted out by not talking to each other, by talking to other people about each other, by an absence of emotion or physical affection, by cheating on each other, and a multitude of other ways. As long as they remain like this, they are in marriage purgatory.

4. Pretending to communicate

There are times when a couple pretends to communicate. One member wants to talk and the other listens and nods as if understanding completely.

Both are pretending. The member who wants to talk doesn't really want to talk, but rather wants to lecture or pontificate and needs the other person to listen and say the right thing. The member who listens doesn't really listen but only pretends to listen in order to appease. "Do you understand what I'm saying?" one member says. "Yes, I understand completely." They go through this ritual now and again, but nothing is really resolved.

For a time, after these pretended talks, things seem to go better. They pretend to be a happy couple. They go to parties and hold hands and everybody remarks on how happy they are. But their happiness is for appearances only. Eventually, the couple falls into the same rut, and there is a need to have another pretended conversation. However, neither partner wants to go deeper into the land of honesty. Pretending is less threatening. And so they live a superficial life.

5. Trying to hurt

In some cases couples can become downright vicious. It is not about being right or winning; it is about inflicting damage on one another. These couples may have initially fallen in love, but down the road they fell in hate. Very often couples who have an alcoholic problem will engage in these kinds of wars, in which they will spend night after night putting each other down, at times in the most vulgar manner. "I don't know why I married a foul-mouthed jerk like you!" one will say, and the other will reply, "You married me because nobody else would take a stupid moron like you."

Obviously, in such marriages communication is at the lowest point. People who argue by putting others down suffer from low self-esteem and are deluded into thinking that by demeaning someone they can be superior in some way. They're on a merry-go-round of discord to distract themselves from the true emptiness of their lives.

COMMUNICATION MISTAKES MADE BY COUPLES

1. Assuming That More Communication Is the Solution

Surprise! You've probably heard before that good communication is the cornerstone of a happy relationship, and, while that might be true, communication alone won't necessarily create that happiness. Sometimes, too much talking could do the reverse.

One of the biggest mistakes is assuming that communication creates connection. For many women, this is often true (talking helps us feel connected to others) but for many men (and for some women), this is not true. It's important to find ways to connect first, before communicating, or else the communication can just generate further feelings of hurt and disconnection. Connecting through a shared activity, acknowledging the efforts the other person makes, or even just being in physical proximity may create the needed connection required to have open and effective communication.

It helps to understand your partner's primary communication style. For example, you may be the type for whom actions speak louder than words; if your partner showers you with compliments but never helps with the household chores, that's a big disconnect. If you and your partner find yourselves always talking things out but still never getting over relationship hurdles, maybe concentrate on other, non-verbal ways to connect.

2. Expecting Your Partner to Read Your Mind

Remember that time your significant other was supposed to do something you wanted but later you found out he or she had no clue? Yup, try as we might, humans aren't great at reading each other's minds. (We have a hard enough time understanding what we do communicate clearly to each other.)

You really can't assume that your spouse knows how you feel or what you want. You don't share the same feelings, worldview or thoughts. You might notice the dishes in the sink or remember that the kids haven't done their homework yet, but he might not. When in doubt, say it out loud.

3. Giving in and Not Really Saying What You Want or Think

If one or both people are averse to conflict, chances are emotions will be buried in the name of pleasing the other person. As someone who's the epitome of conflict avoidance, I can assure you that while that keeps the peace for the short-term, it'll only gradually erode your own happiness and, in turn, the relationship. Power to Change writes:

Some people describe the ideal marriage as a two-way street. If you don't have any arguments, or one side is always directing the traffic, you are riding on a one-way street without any communication. That's not something to cheer about.

4. Harping on (Possibly Hopeless) Issues

The opposite is true as well for couples where both people are stubborn and refuse to compromise. In that case, it's more like a one-lane street with two cars playing chicken with each other. One example of this is what Psychology Today calls the "Woodpecker Syndrome": one person fixates on their feelings and keeps going on and on about it while the other partner withdraws defensively:

One partner is just not willing to give up, continuing toxic conversations and repeating rash lectures.

It does not lead to any constructive dialogue, but a partner affected by the woodpecker syndrome perseveres, as if seeing some invisible "keep going" sign. She becomes a diligent and insensitive lecturer, making forceful monologues that drown in defensive silence. Nothing gets resolved; the relationship deteriorates further. Both partners get exhausted and wary.

This is a communication pattern of ever-diminishing returns. Soon just the mentioning of "let's talk" makes one want to run or hide. A pattern of talking at someone, not to someone, breeds disconnect and widens the relational rift. It does not matter how well-intended the comments are once they are delivered as a bullet point list of suggestions or a stern monotone monologue with no intermissions. Such a way is doomed to just sink in silence and can't serve any good purpose.

5. Not Considering Things from the Other Person's Point of View

Sometimes it's just a matter of being clearer, more upfront, or knowing the best way to communicate with your partner that's at the core of better communication. Equally important, though, is making the effort to understand things from your partner's perspective—something we might not always remember to do. Empathy is the most important skill you can practice, personally and professionally. You don't always have to agree with the other person, but at least you'll both be on the same relationship page.

IMPROVING COUPLES COMMUNICATION

1. Don't accuse. If you're having an issue, be conscious not to point blame at your partner by phrasing sentences that start with words such as "You make me... "or "You didn't..." Instead, begin by saying, "I

feel hurt when..." or "I'm upset when..." Your partner will be less likely to be defensive if you don't sound as though you're in attack mode.

2. Listen. Once you voice what's bothering you, be sure to hear how your partner responds. Give him or her chance to speak and listen to what he or she says. It may be that you're misinterpreting the behavior, he or she wasn't conscious of how you feel, or you're doing or saying something to influence them. Whatever the case may be, unless you hear your partner out, you'll never know.

3. Be consistent. Healthy communication happens during the smallest of moments, not only at meals and when you're on vacation. Speak nicely to your partner and try your best not to let stress or other distractions get the best of you. A devoted husband or wife will want to support you when you need it most, but not if you take your anxiety out on them or take his or her love for granted.

4. Touch often. Communication is not only verbal. Touch your husband or wife often and not only in a sexual way. Hold hands. Kiss him or her hello and goodbye. Let your partner know without words, which people can sometimes misconstrue, just how much he or she means to you. Touching coupled with the right

language can add depth to your relationship that words cannot.

5. Ask questions. Not everyone is forthcoming with information, especially if something is bothering them. Make it a habit of asking your partner how he or she is doing and how his or her day was, even if your spouse is not always interested in speaking with you at length at that exact moment. Expressing that you're interested will go a long way toward keeping the lines free when your partner does want to talk.

6. Remain open. Although it's sometimes more comfortable to stay silent or put off a conversation until later, it's important to resist that temptation. Problems tend to build as opposed to disappearing when we keep issues that are bothering us bottled up inside. If you're having a problem, raise it with your partner, bearing in mind your delivery as I discussed earlier in number one.

7. Compliment your partner. Healthy communication is not only about airing your grievances. It's also about showing your partner just how much you appreciate him or her on both a large and small scale and that you see them. If your husband cooked you a special dinner, acknowledge it. If your wife had her hair done, tell her how lovely she looks. Little

acknowledgments here and there communicate to your partner that, yes, you notice him or her and are happy he or she is a part of your life. Don't hesitate to tell your partner how you're in love and how much he or she means to you. When you do so consistently, chances are, you'll get back what you give and then some by way of the happy marriage you always wanted.

COMMUNICATION SKILLS EVERY COUPLE SHOULD DEVELOP

1. FIND AN OPPORTUNE TIME TO TALK CALMLY ABOUT THE ISSUES.

Preserving time to check in with each other can help you be more productive. Arrange a time in the near future when you are both likely to be calm and comfortable. Perhaps you find that morning tends to work best, or Sunday afternoon when you're in a more relaxed mood. You may need to adjust your schedule slightly so you have some extra time.

Too often, couples attempt to discuss an issue as it's unfolding. While this may work some of the time, giving each other a heads-up to discuss something more in-depth may help you feel more relaxed and open with your partner. Take a moment to express your need and then follow up with a suggestion for a more opportune time. This communicates respect and consideration, which helps to promote an atmosphere of goodwill between two people.

2. UNDERSTAND AND COMMUNICATE YOUR PARTNER'S PERSPECTIVE.

Listening can be tough, especially when the other person is saying something that triggers a defensive response in you. Remind yourself that you will also have a turn; right now it's important to tune in and not interrupt. Make eye contact and be fully present with your partner. You can demonstrate being present by focusing exclusively on the conversation and what's being said. It might be helpful to view the discussion as involving two subjective perspectives rather than one person being "right" or "wrong."

If you're not clear on something, ask a thoughtful question or two to make sure you really understand. You might even say, "Am I getting that right?" or, "I want to make sure I understand; tell me if I'm hearing you correctly ..." Take turns talking and listening to each other. Spending just 10 minutes focused on the other person sharing their perspective can make a significant difference. If you find things are escalating, take a 5-minute break and come back.

3. BE MINDFUL OF YOUR LANGUAGE AND TONE.

When you feel the urge to become accusatory or to begin a statement with "You always ..." stop yourself. Ask yourself what you're feeling in this moment.

It can be so easy to miss an important message when we don't like the tone in which something is being said. Take inventory. When you feel the urge to become accusatory or to begin a statement with "You always ..." stop yourself. Ask yourself what you're feeling in this moment. Taking a minute to slow down before responding can help you say what you truly feel instead of becoming defensive or blaming. Perhaps you might try: "Talking about this always seems to lead us down a destructive path. I'd like to get to a better place with it, but I'm just not sure how." This kind of statement might help to open up a more constructive dialogue.

If you find a particular topic is especially difficult, it may help to share your feelings surrounding the issue. For example, you might say, "I'd really like to talk about (the issue) with you, but I'm feeling anxious about it because I know this is an area we tend to struggle with." Sometimes this sort of statement can relieve the pressure to get it right the first time. Be patient with yourself; with time and practice, communication with your partner can become more productive.

4. THINK IN TERMS OF WHAT YOU CAN GIVE, NOT JUST WHAT YOU CAN TAKE.

While it's certainly true good relationships involve both give and take, when both partners are focused on giving, they strengthen their ability to negotiate conflict more effectively. With some increased awareness, you can shift a problematic dynamic. Tune into your words and actions more carefully. Is there something you can say or do differently to yield different results? When we are kind, we send a caring message to our partner, and when we feel cared for, we can operate from a place of generosity and love.

What positive and unique qualities do you bring to your relationship? What makes you feel happy to provide to your partner? How can you contribute positively to the situation?

5. NOTICE AND SAY OUT LOUD WHAT YOU APPRECIATE ABOUT YOUR PARTNER.

Everyone wants to feel appreciated and valued. It can be easy to fall into a thinking pattern of: "I feel like I do so much, but no one notices." When we take the time to openly appreciate someone else's positive qualities and good deeds, we foster an atmosphere of emotional generosity. Notice something about your partner that you feel grateful for? Share it! Be on the lookout for what you can appreciate and say it. Often, we tend to focus on what we don't have or what's not working in relationships. This critical shift in perspective to a focus on the positive can make all the difference. You might find your partner begins to share their appreciation for how awesome you are as well.

Taking the time to understand your partner's perspective and to reflect back that you truly "get it" can have a significant impact on the quality of your relationship. The next time you find yourself a little stuck, try out the tips above to help you move toward a deeper, more satisfying connection.

COMMUNICATION AND APOLOGY

What Is an Apology?

An apology is a statement that has two key elements:

It shows your remorse over your actions.

It acknowledges the hurt that your actions have caused to someone else.

We all need to learn how to apologize – after all, no one is perfect. We all make mistakes, and we all have the capability to hurt people through our behaviors and actions, whether these are intentional or not.

It isn't always easy to apologize, but it's the most effective way to restore trust and balance in a relationship, when you've done something wrong.

Why Apologize?

There are many reasons why you should make a sincere apology when you've hurt someone unnecessarily, or have made a mistake.

First, an apology opens a dialogue between yourself and the other person. Your willingness to admit your mistake can give the other person the opportunity he needs to communicate with you, and start dealing with his feelings.

When you apologize, you also acknowledge that you engaged in unacceptable behavior. This helps you rebuild trust and reestablish your relationship with the other person. It also gives you a chance to discuss what is and isn't acceptable.

What's more, when you admit that the situation was your fault, you restore dignity to the person you hurt. This can begin the healing process, and it can ensure that she doesn't unjustly blame herself for what happened.

Last, a sincere apology shows that you're taking responsibility for your actions. This can strengthen your self-confidence, self-respect, and reputation. You're also likely to feel a sense of relief when you come clean about your actions, and it's one of the best ways to restore your integrity in the eyes of others.

Consequences of Not Apologizing

What are the consequences if you don't apologize when you've made a mistake?

First, you will damage your relationships with colleagues, clients, friends, or family. It can harm your reputation, limit your career opportunities, and lower your effectiveness – and, others may not want to work with you.

It also negatively affects your team when you don't apologize. No one wants to work for a boss who can't own up to his mistakes, and who doesn't apologize for them. The animosity, tension, and pain that comes with this can create a toxic work environment.

Why Apologies Are Difficult

With all these negative consequences, why do some people still refuse to apologize?

First, apologies take courage. When you admit that you were wrong, it puts you in a vulnerable position, which can open you up to attack or blame. Some people struggle to show this courage.

Alternatively, you may be so full of shame and embarrassment over your actions that you can't bring yourself to face the other person.

Or, you may be following the advice "never apologize, never explain." It's up to you if you want to be this arrogant, but, if you do, don't expect to be seen as a wise or an inspiring leader.

How to Apologize Appropriately

Step 1: Express Remorse

Every apology needs to start with two magic words: "I'm sorry," or "I apologize." This is essential because these words express remorse over your actions.

For example, you could say: "I'm sorry that I snapped at you yesterday. I feel embarrassed and ashamed by the way I acted."

Your words need to be sincere and authentic. Be honest with yourself, and with the other person, about why you want to apologize. Never make an apology when you have ulterior motives, or if you see it as a means to an end.

Timeliness is also important here. Apologize as soon as you realize that you've wronged someone else.

Step 2: Admit Responsibility

Next, admit responsibility for your actions or behavior, and acknowledge what you did.

Here, you need to empathize with the person you wronged, and demonstrate that you understand how you made her feel.

Don't make assumptions – instead, simply try to put yourself in that person's shoes and imagine how she felt.

For example: "I know that I hurt your feelings yesterday when I snapped at you. I'm sure this embarrassed you, especially since everyone else on the team was there. I was wrong to treat you like that."

Step 3: Make Amends

When you make amends, you take action to make the situation right.

Here are two examples:

"If there's anything that I can do to make this up to you, please just ask."

"I realize that I was wrong to doubt your ability to chair our staff meeting. I'd like you to lead the team through tomorrow's meeting to demonstrate your skills."

Think carefully about this step. Token gestures or empty promises will do more harm than good. Because you feel guilty, you might also be tempted to give more than what's appropriate – so be proportionate in what you offer.

Step 4: Promise That It Won't Happen Again

Your last step is to explain that you won't repeat the action or behavior.

This step is important because you reassure the other person that you're going to change your behavior. This helps you rebuild trust   and repair the relationship.

You could say: "From now on, I'm going to manage my stress better, so that I don't snap at you and the rest of the team. And, I want you to call me out if I do this again."

Make sure that you honor this commitment in the days or weeks to come – if you promise to change your behavior, but don't follow through; others will question your reputation and your trustworthiness.

If you're concerned that your words won't come out right when you apologize, write down what you want to say, and then role-play   the conversation with a trusted friend or colleague. However, don't practice so much that your apology sounds rehearsed.

Strategies for Effective Apologies

Keep the following in mind when you apologize.

Don't Offer Excuses

During an apology, many people are tempted to explain their actions. This can be helpful, but explanations can often serve as excuses, and these can weaken your apology. Don't shift part of the blame onto someone or something else in an attempt to reduce responsibility.

Here is an example of using excuses in an apology: "I'm sorry that I snapped at you when you came into my office yesterday. I had a lot on my plate, and my boss demanded my project report an hour earlier than planned." In this case, you excuse your behavior because of stress, and you imply that the other person was at fault because he bothered you on a busy day. This makes you look weak.

A better approach is to say, "I'm sorry I snapped at you yesterday." This is short and heartfelt, and it offers no excuses for your behavior.

Make sure that you are fair to yourself when you make an apology. There is a fine balance between taking full responsibility and taking responsibility for too much.

Don't Expect Instant Forgiveness

Keep in mind that the other person might not be ready to forgive you for what happened. Give that person time to heal, and don't rush her through the process.

For example, after you make your apology, you could say, "I know that you might not be ready to forgive me, and I understand how that feels. I simply wanted to say how sorry I am. I'll give you plenty of time to see that I'm changing my behavior."

Be Aware of Legal Ramifications

Bear in mind that the law in some countries and regions may interpret an apology as an admission of liability or guilt.

Before you apologize on behalf of your organization, you may want to speak with your boss, or get further advice from a legal professional. However, don't use this as an excuse not to apologize, unless the risk is significant.

Be gracious and fair when you receive an apology. If you respond with aggression or self-righteousness, you may lose the respect of the person who apologized, as well as the respect of the people around you.

Don't demand an apology from someone else. They may well refuse, and you can easily end up in an angry, unproductive standoff.

An apology is a statement of remorse that you make when you've done something wrong. It can be difficult to apologize, but it can do a lot to heal relationships and rebuild trust.

Follow these steps when you make an apology:

Express remorse.

Admit responsibility.

Make amends.

Promise that it won't happen again.

Don't offer excuses when you apologize. Otherwise, you'll sound as if you're trying to shift blame away from yourself and on to someone or something else.

HOW TO APOLOGIZE IN A RELATIONSHIP

Apologizing is kind of a crazy, weird thing. You're basically throwing yourself at the mercy of a person you've wronged, and hoping that, for some reason, they decide it's all good. Well, if you apologize like you mean it. Because there's a right and a wrong way to apologize, and just saying "sorry" in a text message won't cut it. No matter how heartfelt you swear your tone was, or how many crying face emoji you use.

Real apologies require digging deep, making yourself vulnerable, and exposing your flaws to another human being. They're also about making amends.

A good apology taps into your skills of communication, empathy, and trust. Even if it's a minor apology, it's still kind of a big deal, in an emotional sense. Plus there's the anxiety of hoping the person you're apologizing to will forgive you, and the task of re-gaining their good favor. These tips will help you smooth things over in a sincere way, but really, if you speak from the heart, and do what feels right, you'll probably do just fine.

Empathy and understanding are practices that allow you to feel from the heart of your partner. To take time to understand your partner's position in a heated debate. Empathy is a difficult skill to master. Yet, it is one that must play a vital role in healthy relationships.

As a way to build your relationship and practice apologizing, take time to understand your partner's needs, wants and concerns. Take time to practice empathy. The more you are able to stop, process and understand the better the relationship will be.

Forgiveness does not mean that you forget. It does not mean that you agree or accept the action. Forgiveness is looking beyond the behavior that took place and trusting that you and your partner can overcome the challenge.

When someone says "I forgive you", it is simply not enough. Forgiveness means that you accept the apology while potentially forgetting or condoning the negative behavior.

Take time to nurture forgiveness by engaging in a conversation. Address the following questions:

What is the definition of forgiveness?

How has the action impacted the relationship?

What steps can I take to address the issue asking for forgiveness?

How can I practice empathy or understanding?

How can we move forward?

As you sit with your partner, hold their hand. Look into each other's eyes and agree to work. To work, each and every day on your relationship. Addressing issues that create tension and creating opportunities for love, intimacy, and lasting love. The important factor to remember is that you are working to create a meaningful experience while showing your significant other that they are valued, needed, wanted, and loved.

1. Dig Deep Into Your Feelings

You need to take a little bit of time to think things over, so you go into your apology with a clear head. You need to know what you did, why you did it, why it upset your partner, and why it might be an issue in your relationship. If you don't think things through, you could go in with some residual anger or resentment and make things even worse. If you've done something knee-jerk, and you know it was immediately wrong, you can immediately apologize, but if it's a serious issue or major relationship crime, take the time to sort it out.

2. Be The Bigger Person

Sometimes you were a little wrong and your partner was also a little wrong. But also sometimes it's important for you to be the bigger person, bite the bullet, and be the one to apologize. It will all come out when you discuss things, and you can have your say about how your partner made you feel. This is a piece of the compromise of being in a relationship. And sometimes your partner will do the same for you. Putting things off too long just gives time for resentment and anger to build.

3. Apologize The Right Way

Once it's time to do the deed, you have to do things right, which means you have to get into full-on apology mode. No phones. No text apologies. No TV in the background. Just you, your partner, and some real eye contact. And then you just have to apologize. Say, "I'm sorry I..." and explain what you're apologizing. This will kick start the discussion and open the door for you both to share your feelings.

4. Listen Like It's Your Job

If you're in a situation where you need to apologize, your partner is going to have some feelings about the situation. Now is the time for you to listen to what they have to say. And not just hear. Really listen. This means tuning in, putting yourself in their shoes, and acknowledging you heard what they said. It's not the time to interrupt or disagree. It's just the time to listen.

5. Make A Plan

If you did something wrong, and you've apologized, that's a great first step, but to really show you mean it, you need to make a plan. This plan can be how to avoid future incidents, how to make amends, or what you can both do to improve your communication skills. If there's a specific problem at hand, you can make a plan to address that. If not, explaining how you understand your partner's point of view and feelings will help them to trust that you meant your apology.

6. Let Your Actions Speak, Too

If you apologize for, say, always being late, and you recognize how it makes your partner feel, and you make a plan to change, you need to follow through. The very next day, you can't be late without a really, really good excuse. Your actions in this situation will speak louder than your words. If you don't follow through, you're not just making your partner mad, but you've crossed the line into violating your partner's trust

7. Buy Presents

I'm kind of joking and kind of not. Of course, you don't need to buy off your partner, and gifts are no excuse for real, healthy communication after a disagreement. But in a time of vulnerability, it can make your partner feel really validated and special if you do something romantic, buy a gift that you know she'll love, make dinner, or do something fun just to lighten the air and bring a little happiness into your lives. Don't mistake this act with your meaningful apology though. It's more of a suggestion than a solution.

NON-VERBAL COMMUNICATION IN A RELATIONSHIP

Communication in a relationship is one of the core essentials that bind individuals together. Since communication is a two-way street, people interact by paying attention when someone talks, and vice-versa.

Good and effective communication makes a successful relationship whether in the personal or professional aspect. But communicating is more than just talking. Apart from the use of words, it is also non-verbal.

In fact, we communicate more with our actions than with words. Nonverbal communication is also known as body language, manifested through facial and body gestures, eye contact, posture, and voice tone.

Remember the cliché 'actions speak louder than words'? There is absolute truth to this proverb. In our interaction with others, our nonverbal cues send a strong message to the person. The way we sit or stand, how we talk, the movement of the arms and eyes are sending off a message that expresses more than verbal cues. In your relationship with other people, the ability to understand and use nonverbal communication is a vital tool in connecting with others, expressing yourself, and building a better connection with the people around you. Depending on how we manifest these nonverbal signals, a sense of interest, trust, and desire to connect will either be developed or not.

Importance of Nonverbal Communication in Marriage

It's true that love, trust, and honesty all play an essential part in building a healthy relationship. However, people often neglect the most crucial part of any relationship which is communication. It plays a vital role in creating a healthy relationship, whether it's verbal or nonverbal communication, your relationship depends on it.

Telling your partner that you love them, again and again, might lose its charm at a certain point. And sometimes you need to express your love and affection without using words, but using different methods of non-verbal communication such as hand signs, facial expressions, and other body gestures. To live a happily married life, you need to learn how to interact with your spouse without a verbal conversation as well.

It's true that sometimes our actions can hurt someone more than our words. Even though you might be listening to what your partner has to say, but by not making eye contact, you may lead them into thinking that what they have to say is of no importance to you, even though that might not be the case!

In simple words, positive or negative body language, maintaining eye contact with your audience, facial expressions, and other bodily gestures are examples of nonverbal communication in relationships. Both verbal and nonverbal communication helps to create and maintain relationships.

Why is nonverbal communication necessary?

Nonverbal communication in a relationship can be incredibly reassuring and understanding the importance of nonverbal communication in relationships can be crucial for the longevity of your marriage/relationship. From a warm smile to a slight touch on the arm are all forms of nonverbal communication that can help in increasing the closeness between you and your significant other.

Such type of interaction plays an essential role in how two people in a relationship can relate with one another. Most of the times we fail to realize that the unconscious mind is powerful and plays a crucial role. It picks up things that might not be that obvious; your unconscious mind is most likely to notice things about other people, what they're doing, their reactions, etc. even though they might not be that obvious.

Body language is another example of nonverbal communication in marriage, a person's posture can tell you a lot about what the other is thinking. There are individuals who can't or don't want to say what they feel. Determining nonverbal cues can help one understand what their spouse is going through.

Nonverbal communication – what you can do

While apologizing, smile a bit to show that you really are sorry. When you see your partner is stressed out, a hug or a light touch on their arm will show them that you're there for them even if they don't wish to talk about it yet.

Make eye contact to show them that you're listening and you think what they have to say is important to you.

Notice what nonverbal cue your partner is giving to you. See if they make eye contact during a conversation. Look at their posture, etc.

The importance of nonverbal communication is undeniable. When you use hand gestures and facial expressions during a conversation, you are trying hard to put forward your point to the others. Another interesting fact about nonverbal communication in marriage or any relationship is that it is easy to catch a liar or a cheater. Their unwillingness to make eye-contacts during conversations, their body language, and hand movements will tell you they are hiding something or simply lying.

Hence, both verbal and nonverbal communication is equally important.

Now, let's understand how you can improve nonverbal communication in romantic relationships like marriage.

1. Express your affection and love

Telling your partner you love them is a great way to keep your marriage happy and healthy. And to do that it's not necessary to say the three words 'I love you' every single time. In fact, you can also express your love through other sweet and kind gestures.

As mentioned earlier, nonverbal communication in marriage involves things such as body language, maintaining eye contact, your facial expressions, and gestures, etc. It's essential that you express affection towards your spouse in a physical, non-sexual way to keep a marriage healthy.

If you aren't able to 'show' how you feel, there's a chance that your spouse might think that you don't truly love them, hence the beginnings of marriage issues. To show your affection toward them, you can make use of simple gestures such as holding their hands or rubbing their shoulders while watching TV, or even giving them an expected hug.

2. Pay attention to each other's mood

A healthy marriage requires you and your partner to pay attention to each other's moods and emotions. People tend to give out quite a lot of cues regarding their mood nonverbally; you must understand these signals to know what's going on in their minds. For example, if they're making a lot of noise while washing the dishes, it might be their way to tell you they're feeling upset about something.

3. Handle disagreements positively

No marriage is free from disagreements. However, you can prevent a disagreement from turning into a full blown out argument. Nonverbal communication plays an essential role in verbal communication. So, when expressing yourself during a disagreement, it's often the words you don't say, but communicate nonverbally that can blow up the situation out of proportion.

That's why it's better to maintain a positive posture during an argument. Rolling your eyes turns your hands into fists, or banging your hand on something won't help you.

4. Surprise them time to time

You can surprise your partner by doing small things, such as leaving sweet notes for them to read, getting or making little gifts for them, buying flowers, cooking dinner or by simply doing their share of the chores. There are a lot of ways you can communicate your feelings and affections without speaking a word. This is why nonverbal communication is important.

So, give the above-mentioned nonverbal communication in marriage points a try. It might take time to perfect them, but with enough devotion you'll be able to strengthen your marital relationship with both verbal and nonverbal interaction.

Types of Non-Verbal Communication

There are many different types of non-verbal communication. They include:

Body movements (kinesics), for example, hand gestures or nodding or shaking the head, which are often the easiest element of non-verbal communication to control;

Posture or how you stand or sit, whether your arms are crossed, and so on;

Eye contact, where the amount of eye contact often determines the level of trust and trustworthiness;

Para-language or aspects of the voice apart from speech, such as pitch, tone, and speed of speaking;

Closeness or personal space (proxemics), which determines the level of intimacy, and which varies very much by culture;

Facial expressions, including smiling, frowning and blinking, which are very hard to control consciously. Interestingly, the broad facial expressions that show strong emotions, such as fear, anger, and happiness, are the same throughout the world; and

Physiological changes, for example, you may sweat or blink more when you are nervous, and your heart rate is also likely to increase. These are almost impossible to control consciously and are therefore a very important indicator of mental state.

Using Non-Verbal Communication

Non-verbal communication helps people to:

Reinforce or modify what is said in words.

For example, people may nod their heads vigorously when saying "Yes" to emphasize that they agree with the other person. A shrug of the shoulders and a sad expression when saying "I'm fine, thanks" may actually imply that things are not really fine at all!

Convey information about their emotional state.

Your facial expression, your tone of voice and your body language can often tell people exactly how you feel, even if you have hardly said a word. Consider how often you have said to someone,

"Are you OK? You look a bit down."

We know how people feel from their non-verbal communication.

Define or reinforce the relationship between people.

If you have ever watched a couple sitting talking, you may have noticed that they tend to 'mirror' each other's body language. They hold their hands in similar positions, they smile at the same time, and they turn to face each other more fully. These movements reinforce their relationship: they build on their rapport, and help them to feel more connected.

Provide feedback to the other person.

Smiles and nods tell someone that you are listening and that you agree with what they are saying. Movement and hand gestures may indicate that you wish to speak. These subtle signals give information gently but clearly.

Regulate the flow of communication

There are a number of signals that we use to tell people that we have finished speaking, or that we wish to speak. An emphatic nod and firm closing of the lips indicates that we have nothing more to say, for example. Making eye contact with the chair of a meeting and nodding slightly will indicate that you wish to speak.

Tips to Improve Non-Verbal Communication for a Happier Relationship

You probably know that effective verbal and non-verbal communication is an important part of any happy, committed relationship.

But, did you realize that 93% of your communication with your partner is non-verbal?

Non-verbal cues include body language such as posture, muscle tension, eye contact, facial expressions, gestures, actions, decisions, breathing, attitude and tone of voice.

Since non-verbal communication is such a significant part of the interpersonal dynamic between you and your partner, focusing your efforts here is the key to increasing closeness, building understanding and promoting trust between the two of you.

Be Affectionate – Hold hands, hug and always kiss hello and goodbye

Smile Lovingly – A genuine smile conveys happiness with your relationship

Be Patient – Cultivate an attitude of acceptance

Play Together – Be your partner's recreational companion

Be Flirtatious – Use your eyes to show desire and admiration

Create Rituals – Share a cup of coffee and have a weekly date night

Listen Attentively – Give your full, undivided attention

Be Thoughtful – Leave a surprise note or small gift for your partner to find

Show Devotion – Put your phone away when you spend time together

Greet Warmly – Show excitement and joy on the phone/text and in person

SEXUAL COMMUNICATION IN A RELATIONSHIP

Understanding how couples communicate about sex is another indicator of sexual and relationship satisfaction.

Sexual communication is defined as the communication and self-disclosure and communication processes around sexual topics and problems. The distinction between sexual communication and regular couple communication comes from the assumption that sexual communication entails a great deal of inherent

116

vulnerability. While couples may feel comfortable talking about a number of issues and topics in their relationship, they may have difficulty discussing the topic of sexuality.

Communication about sex may differ from general couples' communication because of various social or cultural reasons. The comfort level discussing sexuality within a couple may be due to social/cultural norms, individual experiences, or relational patterns. Sex may commonly be considered taboo due to social and cultural influences. Individuals may view talking about sex as inappropriate or even embarrassing. Partners may have different opinions about discussing sexuality, due to differing expectations, desires, experiences, or beliefs, which in turn may affect the relationship. Some may have

Sexual trauma that may influence attitudes toward sex. In any case, communicating specifically about one's own sexual relationship entails a great level of vulnerability, which may make it difficult to make adjustments in the sexual relationship if needed.

This vulnerability may make it difficult for couples to discuss sexual preferences, passions, and desires. Beyond the need to make adjustments, sexual communication has a number of other influences on relationship and sexual satisfaction.

There is a burgeoning body of research showing that higher disclosure to one's partner about sexual preferences and desires is positively correlated with sexual satisfaction and relationship quality. However, while the amount sexual self-disclosure may have a positive impact on the relationship.

What we lack is a clearer understanding of how sexual communication influences long-term relationships.

Each of these constructs are difficult to measure independent of one another because they all effect, and are affected by, each other. Thus, understanding how each of these components is related is crucial to developing a clearer picture of the state of a relationship. This study focuses on two different types of sexual communication: content and process. Sexual communication content focuses on the breadth and depth of sexual topics discussed while sexual communication process have more to do with the relational patterns in discussing sexual topics.

Sexual Communication - Why is it Important for Couples?

Communication in any relationship is indispensable for creating a strong bond between a couple and a part of that communication is communicating about your desires and fantasies.

Sexual Communication is when you and your partner are able to express your needs and wants without the conversation being awkward, taking in account what the other feels. It is a fulfilling, satisfying, and a fun part of life. The physical aspect of love is an important part of a relationship and communicating with your partner about it only helps to make it better. Sexual communication will make it easier for you to take pleasure in sex with safety and have a satisfying sex life.

Physical Communication: Communication is not linked with words only. Sometimes, a gentle hand placed on your shoulder or back, a simple glance at you or even a wink are enough to lure someone towards you. Healthy and amazing sexual activity is procured mainly through physical intimacy. Almost all the time, couples find out what the other is thinking even without asking them. 'Actions speak louder than words' is proven to be very true in this case. So, ensure that you understand physical cues of each other.

Sexual Directions: Giving your partner verbal or physical direction is an integral part of achieving a satisfied sexual life. He or she needs to be informed of where to touch you and where not to in order to turn you on. If your spouse is clueless of what you might want or expect in bed, sexual gratification will not only become impossible but may turn disastrous. If there is verbal communication between you two such as, 'kiss me' or 'touch me there', the sexual experience will become ten times better. This happens only when there is love and proper sexual communication.

Conversational Communication: Sexual urge is aroused only when there is vocal communication. All relationships require good oral communication. Communication related to sex must be done tactfully without making it awkward or uncomfortable. It will help solve many issues in your sexual and love life. You must focus on what your partner might prefer doing more or may work around issues which cause strife and eventually resolve them.

Intimacy: Emotional as well as sexual intimacy requires honest communication. Some display their inner inhibitions while others are reserved in matters of expression on sexual life. Each couple is accustomed to different and unique styles of communication with their partners. It is important to be able to comfortably and smoothly express yourself and get instant feedback from your spouse in order to be most compatible with each other. If you wish to discuss about any specific sexual problem, you can consult a sexologist and ask a free question.

How Sexual Communication Differs From Nonsexual Communication

One sign of a healthy long-term romantic relationship is frequent sexual communication. Studies have consistently found that the more sexual communication couples engage in, the more sexually satisfied they tend to be. Despite the well-documented and powerful role that sexual communication plays in our relationships, surprisingly little research has explored in detail how we tend to navigate sexual discussions.

It is vital that we study sexual communication because by considering how people feel about and approach it, we can come to understand why some people avoid sexual communication altogether, as well as how we might help struggling couples facilitate more effective communication in their own relationships.

As the researchers predicted, participants displayed more warmth when discussing a sexual conflict compared to a nonsexual conflict, which suggests that people seem to be more responsive to one another when talking about sex compared to other relationship matters.

Levels of warmth varied more during the sexual discussion relative to the nonsexual discussion; however, this was only true for women. The authors of the study believe this may be because people tend to adjust their warmth more when discussing sensitive subjects like sex in order to manage their partner's emotional experience.

Unexpectedly, there were no differences in levels of dominance displayed in the sexual and nonsexual scenarios. The researchers expected to find that people would display less dominance during sexual conflicts, but that clearly wasn't the case.

Levels of dominance varied less in the sexual discussion relative to the nonsexual discussion, which suggests that people may be more cautious in the way they approach sexual conversations.

When one partner displayed warmth, the other tended to respond in kind. In other words, warmth was greeted with warmth. However, this tendency emerged more often in sexual versus nonsexual conflicts.

When one partner displayed dominance, the other tended to respond in a reciprocal way. This means that dominance was typically greeted with submissiveness. However, this pattern emerged more often in nonsexual compared to sexual conflicts.

Participants said they felt more anxious prior to discussing a sexual conflict than a nonsexual conflict.

Overall, these results reveal a lot about the nature of sexual communication and how it is similar to and different from nonsexual communication. The pattern of findings suggests that people tend to see higher stakes when discussing sexual conflicts, which may be why a lot of us avoid talking about sex altogether, but also why we seem to approach sexual communication more cautiously than nonsexual communication.

Ways to Start Sexual Communication

Being intimate with your partner can seem like a created thing but can sometimes be too complicated.

Most couples wonder about why it isn't easy and why their partners refuse to be on the same frequency as they are. Why is it that married life does not look like a Nicholas Sparks novel and your intimate moments are not steamy enough?

It is important for husband and wife to be able to talk about their bedroom affairs and other things openly.

Sometimes it may feel as if you both are worlds apart, but during this time it is important to talk things out.

Without communication, you may miss out the best parts of marriage such as closeness intimacy and the joy. If your love life is good, then don't forget to appreciate your husband and how he treats you. If things are going downhill then sit down and discuss your problems and take a chance to open up a sexual conversation.

1. Understand that both genders respond and think differently

Even though male sexuality and thinking are often discussed in our community as a norm but when it comes to women, it is easy to assume that something is wrong with her. The basis of good communication relies on how normal you think the response of you and your partner is.

If the wife does not respond well to her husband, people naturally assume there is something bad about her.

Both partners have different sexual responses; women need time to get in the mood whereas men sometimes get incredibly frustrated.

Understand these responses and communicate accordingly.

2. Find out what's bothering you

Before you sit down and talk to your partner, spend some time alone figuring out what bothers them and what has gotten them all frustrated.

There might be a sexual problem, the problem in the marriage, time problem or something else. Once you figure out what it is trying to fix it.

It may be difficult for the two of you to figure it out so spend some time clearly thinking about it and then make amends.

3. Own up for your mistake

When sexual problems are concerned most partners refuse to acknowledge their contribution to the problem. It is smart to stand up for the mistakes you've made and to acknowledge them even if you think your partner is responsible.

The entire purpose of this communication is to find a solution to the problem arising between you two and moving past it. Avoid blaming one another.

4. Say what you want

This can be very hard, especially for women.

Women think as if it is not ladylike to communicate what level of intimacy they want and this is what gives birth to misunderstanding.

Women like to believe that their men know exactly what they need and so what they actually need keeps floating in their minds, confusing them.

Sometimes men avoid talking about their preferences as they feel it may upset their spouse. This is where everything goes wrong; both partners should have enough level of trust in one another that they are able to communicate openly.

Work on changing your thoughts and gather up the courage to be able to openly discuss the problems in your marriage.

5. Open up the conversation

Choose a time where both of you are not stressed out or worried and start up the conversation.

Let your partner know that the goal of this is increased intimacy and share what you are feeling and thinking. Encourage your partner to do this too.

This step may be too hard for some people, but it will help improve your relationship. Keep in mind that if you don't communicate then the conversation cannot begin.

6. Keep on going

It is important that once your conversation starts towards intimacy that you let it all out.

Many problems in sexual intimacy do not get fixed overnight and need time in getting solved. Sometimes it can take couples a long while to be able to talk through their problems and have good communication.

The key to fixing these glitches is to let your partner know everything wrong with you two; do not hold up. Be kind instead of being harsh.

Having sexual issues in a relationship is pretty normal. However, it is important that both the partners sit down and discuss these issues.

Communicate openly about things as this will help in strengthening your marriage and be a good foundation for the future. Avoid blaming one another and move forward to having stronger intimacy with kind and honest words.

How To Talk About Sex With Your Partner To Keep The Spark Alive

Unfortunately, we live in a culture that still shames having sex for pleasure.

"A few others feel intimidated about sex in general and can't fathom discussing it with their partners. People will avoid talking to their partners about what they want in bed because they fear embarrassment and/or rejection."

It's also important to keep in mind that your individual tastes and preferences can change over time. So if you're in a long-term relationship keeping the lines of communication open is important, especially if you want to keep having amazing sex. So how do you get to that point?

1. Trust Your Partner

Fear over being judged can make you hesitate. "Don't be shy! Trust, respect, and openness should be at the foundation of your relationship, so telling your partner what you want sexually can be an honest process without fear of judgment."

If you can trust that your partner won't judge you in any other aspect of your life, it's important to trust they won't judge you when it comes to sex.

2. Approach It With Curiosity

An easy way to introduce the topic is by staying curious. You can say something like, I'm curious about how you think our sex life is, and if there is anything you're missing or want to try. "Coming from a place of curiosity will help them to be forthright rather than defensive". "If they say something that rings true with you, that's an opportunity to connect and share your own preferences and desires. Most of the time this conversation prompts another fantastic chapter in a couple's sex life."

3. Bring It Up In A Neutral Location Like It's NBD

"It's as simple and as difficult as that". Strike up a conversation in a neutral location like on a car ride, while grocery shopping, or while walking the dog. That way no one feels pressured to answer in a certain way. If you bring it up in the middle of sex, for instance, the added pressure on your partner may make them uncomfortable.

"Keeping the lines of communication open regarding sex ensures that everyone is on the same page and feels safe enough to voice their opinions when things come up". "Remember, your partner is not a mind reader." So don't be afraid to just go for it.

4. Use A Checklist To Share Your Fantasies

"Sharing fantasies and desires is the best way to keep the spark alive" "You will have much better sex if you actually know what a partner wants, doesn't want and isn't sure about." If you need guidance, she suggests using a checklist like this one.

Healthy communication is key to spicing things up while maintaining safety. Jealousy and insecurity can emerge if we don't do a good job of knowing ourselves and our partner. For instance, if someone has been cheated on and still hurts from it, swinging probably wouldn't be the right suggestion. But maybe reading erotic literature or watching a sexy video together in bed can spark a new interest.

"We all get into routines and patterns and if we never pull from our imaginations, someone is bound to get bored".

5. Find Fun And Creative Ways To Bring It Up

If using a checklist, such as the one above, isn't your thing, there are plenty of other ways to spark a conversation about likes, dislikes, and interests. For example, watching a movie or your favorite show together and asking your partner what they think about a certain scenario can help shed light on how they feel about certain acts. Playing a sex game or using position cards can be fun, light ways to start talking. You can even create a coupon book to give to your significant other filled with ideas you want to explore and include some blank ones for them to fill in.

6. Always Use Positive Words, Especially When You're Working Out An Issue

Opening up about fantasies isn't the only reason to talk about sex. If you have trouble climaxing with your partner, it's important to bring that up as well. If you want to open up communication because of a critique or an issue, it's important to emphasize the positive. Instead of focusing on what they're doing wrong, focus on what you want.

"As a basic rule to try is to use a compliment sandwich whenever you are discussing a potentially delicate subject". You can trying saying something like, I love the way you touch me. I'd love it if you touched me more. You're great. "Try to offer solutions and always keep things positive. This is your intimate partner after all and beneficial sharing can make your relationship even better."

7. Give Each Other Permission To Share Without Judgment

If you're openly expressing what you want to try or what you want more of in bed, it's important to let your partner know that they can — and should — do the same.

If want to have better sexual communication in your relationship, you should give each other permission to share without judgment. "This is the most important step because it will allow for the process of sharing". "Permission is a powerful thing."

Opening up about sex is a process, and it doesn't need to happen overnight. But as long as you say the words and follow through with actions, there's no reason your sex life shouldn't reap the rewards.

THINGS TO IMPROVE SEX COMMUNICATION

Good sex is a multi-sensory experience that brings connection, closeness, pleasure and intimacy between two or more consenting people. When you think about sex, the physical act is usually what comes to mind. Sex that is portrayed in movies, on television or in porn suggests that you intuitively know how to turn your partners on. However, in reality, if you don't talk about it, you won't know. Sex can be fraught with a range of emotions, complicated histories, and assumptions.

Additionally engaging in the physical act is only part of what makes for good sex. Good sex communication is essential in order for it to be satisfying, healthy, and safe. Talking about sex helps you and your partner(s) connect and learn about each other. Because of this, below you will find four things to consider that will improve your sexual communication and make your sex even better!

1. Say Yes to what you want and No to what you don't

Express your sexual desires and interests so that your partner(s) know how to please you. Tell them what you like and what you don't. What kinds of sexual activities do you enjoy? Are you willing to try that you haven't done? What are you not willing to do?

2. Non-verbal sex communication

Non-verbal communication is an important part of any sexual experience. However, you don't want to only rely on non-verbal communication during sex. Non-verbal communication can be easily misinterpreted. Awareness of your partner's response to your touch is an example of non-verbal sexual communication. Other ways you can communicate during sex can include cuing in to receptive body movements, breathing, moans, or sighs. Attention to non-verbal cues can keep you attuned to your partner during sex.

3. Talk with partners about sex to increase sexual safety and informed decision-making

Sex that is portrayed in the media and online often don't include conversations about health status and sexual history. Talking openly about sex and desire can sometimes be an unfamiliar or difficult experience. You may feel uncomfortable, self-conscious, or vulnerable, especially if you are sharing sexual trauma or health status. Questions to ask your partners might include: What kind of touch do you like? Are there parts of your body where you don't want to be touched? What kind of barriers do you use? Are there sexual activities you are willing to enjoy without barriers? Are you using birth control? Because our relationship to sex is complex and multi-faceted, it's okay to feel some nervousness or hesitation. Move at your own pace. Take the time to talk openly about sex to increase safety and comfort.

4. Increase comfort and intimacy

Healthy sexual communication will allow you and your partners to feel more comfortable pleasing each other. As a result, you may feel closer and better able to connect. When you feel safe and connected, you will develop a deeper understanding of each other's desires and strengthen your relationships. You will learn and understand the kind of sexual relationships you want to have with one another.

Remember that sex communication is a skill that requires practice and feedback. Furthermore you may initially find your style of communication awkward and clunky. Because of this remember to ask questions; get feedback; learn about each other's histories and desires and cue into non-verbal communication. In addition to better communication, practice will increase your skills and will ease future sex communication, sexual satisfaction, health, and connection.

SIGNS OF POOR COMMUNICATION IN A RELATIONSHIP

There are a few signs of poor communication that you should pay attention to, if you think it's the cause of the problems in your relationship. We're all human and we all make mistakes, and that's why you need to learn to solve disagreements that you might have with your partner - so you'll be able to overcome successfully any obstacle that may appear in your path. Here are a few signs of poor communication in your relationship that you should consider:

NOT LISTENING

This is one of the most obvious signs of poor communication in every relationship. The fact that someone always cuts off their partner every time they speak, can send a wrong message to that person; for example that their opinion and their thoughts are insignificant. Just try to improve your listening skills and always try to understand what your partner is telling you because this is one of the best ways to prevent any misunderstanding.

BEING PASSIVE AGGRESSIVE

Passive aggressiveness is one of the most dangerous forms of communication because by using it, you can really hurt the other person and in the long term, this type of behavior can really affect the stability of your relationship. If you remain calm during an argument, try to use your words to sort things out and not to hurt the other person.

LOSING YOUR TEMPER VERY EASILY

If you have anger issues and if you easily lose your temper, then you might have communication problems too. The anger will not allow you to express yourself rationally and your behavior may hurt your partner's feelings. Despite this, everyone is accountable for their actions and for their reactions, so try to solve this problem in order to improve the communication in your relationship.

NAGGING

Yes, nagging is indeed a sign of poor communication in your relationship. If someone constantly follows their partner yelling at them or repeating the same demands over and over again, they will not manage to communicate more efficiently and their partner will not receive the message they are trying to send either. Just learn some communication techniques and solve the problems in your relationship in a more healthy way.

IGNORING

Ignoring your partner is not a way to improve the communication in your relationship. Not talking to your partner when you are upset over something they did is never a good solution if you want to solve that problem. Ignoring your partner will only cause more problems in your relationship and you will only sabotage yourself and your happiness.

USING BAD LANGUAGE

Even if you're upset, this doesn't give you the right to offend or to hurt your partner. Don't use profanities, and be respectful! After all, you are talking about the person you love, so be a bit more empathetic and a bit more caring when you are dealing with them.

BEING ARGUMENTATIVE

Of course, every couple fights sometimes because we are all different, so it's only natural to disagree on certain things. Yet, you should try to learn how to fight in a friendly manner, so that your arguments can be more productive. Don't use insults and be respectful!

Because relationships do require a bit of work and because everyone makes mistakes sometime, we should all try to constantly improve the communication in our relationships, so we'll all be able to live happier and healthier lives.

EARLY RELATIONSHIP PROBLEMS

It's often tough to spot potential relationship problems when you're in the throes of a new love. Heck, you might even see a red flag or two, but not care one bit because woo this is so much fun! I totally get it, and yet that doesn't mean you should ignore early relationship problems, especially since many have of a way of getting worse with time.

So do yourself a favor. If you notice something that seems a bit off — maybe your partner is controlling, or you two always argue — don't look the other way. "Everyone is usually on their best behavior in the beginning of a relationship". "Whatever red flags or differences appear early on, remember they will only get worse. Whatever behaviors might be an issue for you, try to imagine them heightened down the line, and ask if you can live with that."

You can give your new partner the benefit of the doubt, and take some time to work on things. "Perhaps they can control the negative behavior".

"But, in cases where ... there are some incompatibilities from the beginning, it's probably best to fold and move on, because that is not going to get better."

1. A Lack Of Sexual Chemistry

If you two aren't the most sexually compatible, you can definitely work on it by communicating and experimenting. And over time, you may find your groove and start to have great sex. But if there seems to be no chemistry whatsoever, keep in mind this problem doesn't always work itself out — especially if you aren't willing to talk about it.

"The beginning of a relationship, when a couple is in the honeymoon stage, is the time when fireworks should be going off every time they are together". "If that chemistry is not there from the beginning, it usually will only go downhill from there."

Of course, sex isn't everything in a relationship, and it's always possible to have a healthy relationship, without this being one of the main pillars. You just have to decide what's important to you, and communicate all of that to your partner.

2. Having Nothing In Common

While you two don't have to be twins, it may not be a good idea to force a relationship with someone who's your total opposite. Because, "if there is just no common ground, it will likely lead to the couple eventually having separate lives."

If you're an extrovert and they're an introvert, for example, or if you like to hike and they won't even step outside, such differences can cause you to spend too much time apart, possibly to the point where you don't see each other often enough. It can also become frustrating, if these things are important to you and not your partner, or vice versa. But again, it's about focusing on what's important to you. While a problem may not ever go away, that doesn't necessarily mean it has to ruin your relationship.

3. A Controlling And Demanding Personality

People are normally on their best behavior in the early days of a relationship, where they want to impress and put their best foot forward. So don't ignore any red flags that your partner might be controlling or demanding, or other signs of a toxic personality.

"These will not only get worse, but could also ... foreshadow a potentially abusive partner." It can help to point out certain bad habits to your partner early on, as a way of communicating about them. It's possible they don't even realize how they're coming off, or the impact they're having on you.

You may also want to go to couples therapy, as a way of working through issues. But if the relationship is one that doesn't feel healthy, and it seems like you've tried everything, it may be time to accept the problem isn't going away, and it's time to move on.

4. Different Spending Habits

Since money is one of the top things couples fight about, don't be surprised if this becomes your go-to argument, especially if it's been a problem since day one. If you don't see eye-to-eye in terms of things like how to split a restaurant bill, that can be an early red flag. But from there, differing opinions can begin to impact things like your household bills, rent, and so on.

"Since [money is] such a crucial aspect in day-to-day life ... understanding how both you and your [partner] relates to it is important". "Don't wreck a relationship just because you are stressed about money and don't like or respect the way your partner handles it." Instead, talk about it — before it gets out of hand.

5. Issues From The Past

Any fights about family members or ex partners will likely only get more heated, so you'll want to nip those in the bud ASAP. If you notice early on that you are not on the same page when dealing with things from the past, you need to begin talking right away about what's OK and what isn't.

It may help to sit down and have a serious conversation about boundaries, what's safe to talk about, and how you plan to deal with this issue should it come up again. If you both respect each other's opinions, this problem doesn't have to get worse.

6. Boundary Issues

Unclear relationship boundaries almost always lead to resentment, which is something that can get worse with time — for you and your partner.

"While we all want to love others 'no matter what,' we must first love ourselves and establishing healthy boundaries and standards is the best thing we can do". Once you do that, you'll have a better shot a healthy relationship.

This might look like talking about how much time to spend together versus how much time to spend apart, and what you'd both like to get out of the relationship. Knowing early on can save you from having arguments and misunderstandings years down the road.

7. An Inability To Communicate

Open and honest communication is something you'll have to work on throughout your entire relationship. And even the healthiest couples will have ups and downs, and moments where they don't "get" each other.

That said; if communication doesn't feel at least relatively easy right out of the gate, things will probably only get worse. "Poor communication habits eventually harm the relationship." You can't create a healthy connection if you aren't listening to each other, for example, or respecting each other's opinions.

This is something you can work on, possibly again by going to therapy. But simply prioritizing healthier communication can be a big help, too.

8. Disrespect And Dishonesty

If someone can't be respectful on the first date, imagine how they'll act on the 100th. This may not be something you want to wait around for, especially if their behavior is particularly bad.

"If you notice a wandering eye or words and actions not matching up and your gut simply says 'this doesn't feel right,' pay close attention". They're probably not the most trustworthy person, and that's one trait can lead to a lot of problems in the future.

9. Cheating

A wandering eye is one thing. But if you think your partner might cheat, or if they're giving off signs that they already are, run far away and save yourself.

"Infidelity is typically the most destructive problem in a relationship and signals major problems". The cheating itself isn't even the biggest problem, but the fact it's rooted in all sorts of trust and respect issues.

And that's not something many people can magically change about themselves, unless they show you they're really committed to trying.

10. Financial Secrets

It's not uncommon to downplay financial issues in the first few months of dating. People want to make a good first impression, and you probably won't find yourself talking about finances on a first date. But that doesn't mean it's healthy to hide this part of yourselves forever.

If you or your partner have a lot of debt, bad spending habits, or a poor credit score — just to name a few financial issues — you'll want to let each other know. "These issues always surface at some point". "The trust that is lost spills over into distrust in other areas."

11. Trust Issues

Speaking of trust issues, once trust is broken it's often really hard to get it back. And that's because "trust is the foundation of all relationships". So even if something seems small at first, it can grow and spread, he says, and get worse over time.

While it may take a while to create a secure relationship, pay attention to small betrayals of trust early on in the relationship. If it seems like a pattern, it may be one that isn't going to go away.

12. Ineffectual Arguing

Communication issues can get worse as time goes on. And the same is true for ineffectual arguing styles. "Couples need good communication skills, and this is especially true during conflict". "If you don't do it well during the early stages of your relationship, it will continue to be a problem during the course of your relationship as life gets more complicated and challenging."

If you happen to notice that you aren't understanding each other, or seeing eye-to-eye, bring it to each other's attention ASAP. This may help you argue in a healthier way, so things don't become more toxic going forward.

While it's always possible to work on bad habits, keep in mind that some issues can get worse with time, and especially if they're turning into a pattern. The sooner you can notice these mistakes and start making changes, the better your relationship will be.

WAYS TO KEEP YOUR RELATIONSHIP TOGETHER THROUGH THE HARD TIMES

Every relationship go through hard times, learn how to strengthen yours through the hard times

You might find yourself with a death in the family, a financial hardship or a crisis that keeps you up at night, it is these hard times that can make your relationship stronger. It may seem hard at first. It is the hard times that can bring the best out of people.

Every relationship experiences some hard times. It is the stressful occurrences that can bring your relationship to a new level of strengthening your love and understanding for one another.

154

Hard times can create a great opportunity for your commitment for one other to be unshaken and unmovable to bring you closer together. In order, for you to strengthen your relationship, there must be communication involved. Communicating is crucial to the relationship. Having the ability to communicate freely and on-going will build a stronger relationship. Here are five ways you can keep it together through the hard times.

Talk It Out

Telling your partner how you feel is vital to your relationships. This expression should be done out of respect. Speak to them out of love, the same way you want to be spoken to. This way will better receive from them. Telling your partner how you feel will benefit the relationships. There is no way they will know how you feel if you don't tell them, most likely cannot read your mind. The worst you want to do is be demanding or condescending to where you are more like a dictator rather than an equal partner.

Avoiding any hard topics can create more stress in your life. Burying your feelings underneath only will explode up like a raging bull. By talking it out, it allows you to open up and become more intimate with your feelings which in return draws you closer to your partner. Once you grow closer, you will form a new level of appreciation for one other.

Validate Their Feelings

Being heard and be present in a relationship is essential to its well-being. Not having your voice heard in your relationship is just as bad as the old saying that many of us grew up with hearing, "Children are to be seen and not heard." When you shut the door on their voice, you loss great opportunities to grow closer and build a stronger lasting relationship.

Everyone wants to be treated as number one, especially in their relationships. Validating and respecting their feelings will give a sense of belonging. This validation is done by listening. Once you take the time to listen and not anticipate your rebuttal, this will allow you to pay attention and be more involved in the conversation. Validating one's feelings do not mean you have to agree with them, but you should respect them. Remember that being right is not always right in every situation.

Agree To Disagree

There is no person the same. We are all made up different which makes us unique. We might have some very common similarity, but at the end of the day, we are different. Being different doesn't mean we shouldn't get alone, it is the opposite. Being different should draw us together to want to learn from each other.

Agreeing to disagree and acknowledge different opinions is a must in relationships. Agree to come to a solution where you both can be happy. Having patience and understanding go hand and hand with resolving and conflict. Don't allow yourself to fall into the trap that things have to be done one way only. If there is a need to apologize, quickly apologize. Apologizing is a sign of strength, and it clears the air of any false perfection.

Take A Break

It can be challenging to hold a conversation if the discussion is not moving towards a solution. Instead of the constant back and forth dialogue only feeling more like a heated tennis match where no one is winning, take a break. It is essential to take a break especially if you find yourself still not on the same page.

Taking a break will give you and your partner a better chance to reflect on the discussion. Most of the time we can find ourselves only seeing one side of the conversation, which it just gets impossible to see another way. Taking a break does not have to be wrong. It gives you and your partner the opportunity to see a different perspective.

Laying The Foundation

Remember why you are with your partner. Remember what drawn you together. Remember the best moments together such as how you met, the first date, the first time you said "I love you," and the moment you knew this was the person for you. It is easy to lose focus on the crucial things due to the negativity that can occur in our lives but looking at the positivity can revive the relationship to a new level of togetherness.

Weighing the good memories verse the conflicts will determine how serious you are committed to fighting for your relationship. There are certain situations where you may feel like your back is against the wall and the only decision is to give up. But more often than not, once you see and remember the foundation of your relationship, you can decide that it is worth fighting for your relationship.

Accept that Disappointment Will Happen in every Relationship.

Disappointment happens when our expectations don't match reality. Two people will always have differences in their expectations. This means that disappointments will happen in every relationship. We have a tendency to focus on the negative and we then use this "evidence" to reinforce the belief that our relationships are filled with disappointment. Instead, accept that disappointment happens. Choose to focus on the parts that have fulfilled your expectations and even brought unplanned blessings.

Don't Stonewall.

Stonewalling is a passive-aggressive tactic that may seem neutral, but is very damaging. Whenever you ignore, stall, and refuse to participate, you are stonewalling. It is a power-play intended to break down the opposition. It keeps the relationship in a "me versus you" dynamic. For a relationship to survive, it must be an "us against the world" commitment.

Don't Make Derogatory Comments, Insults & Belittling Remarks.

The words you use are powerful. When you put down your partner or your relationship, you are causing damage. Choose to break habits that damage the relationship, especially when you feel frustrated and disappointed. Use words that show respect, love, and hope. Plant the seeds you want to grow.

Don't Play the Blame Game.

This is a game no one wins. Even if you are successful in blaming all your problems on your partner, you still are stuck with all those problems and the feelings that come with them. The only way to begin transforming your problems into solutions is to take full responsibility for the parts you play. Stop blaming and start creating the relationship you want.

Focus on the Qualities You Love & Respect in Your Partner.

Remember the moments and reasons why this person became special and important to you. Trust that all those things are still true. Close your eyes and hold those moments in your heart. Allow yourself to feel again the love, pride, and respect that you felt. Return to these moments to revitalize your commitment to strengthen your relationship.

Believe That Your Partner Has Good Intentions.

Psychological studies have proven that once we become convinced of an idea, our brain will ignore and discredit information that contradicts what we believe. When we are feeling hurt and disappointed, we have a tendency to turn our partner into the villain. But if your relationship is going to have a chance to turn around, you must make room for the possibility that your partner can be your greatest ally. Believe that your partner has good intentions, but the information he/she is acting on is incorrect or the impact is hurtful.

Learn How to Forgive.

We have many misunderstandings about what forgiveness means. Forgiveness does not mean you give permission for someone to mistreat you. It means that you accept that we are all doing the best we can. Surely if we knew better, we would do better. When we disappoint and hurt each other, it's not because we want to. Forgive that your partner hasn't learned better ways of loving you YET. Forgiveness means you commit to letting go of the hurt of the past to allow for new possibilities in the future.

**Make it Clear That You Want to Hear &
Understand Your Partner.**

Tell your partner, "I know in the past I may have not done a good job of listening to you. I see that this has hurt you and me. I must not fully understand what is going on. I want to. I want to understand who you are and what matters to you. I will keep listening as long as it takes."

Ask Your Partner to Share.

Ask, "Are you willing to share with me? Whenever you're ready to share, I'm ready to hear. And I will wait until you feel safe," then practice being fully present.

Learn What Needs to Happen for Your Partner to Feel Loved & Respected.

We all have different rules for what needs to happen for us to feel loved and respected. Some people need to be told "I love you" many times every day. Others need to have one-on-one time for at least twenty minutes each day. A hand pat from time to time will suffice for others. Ask your partner, "What makes you feel loved? What have I done that has made you feel close to me? What do I do that lets you know I'm proud of you?" Then give your partner what he/she needs as frequently as they need it.

Learn About Your Damaging Cycles.

Partners can fall into damaging patterns. A common pattern is the pursuer/withdrawer cycle. One partner will attack, nag, or chatter in a way to provoke a reaction from the other. Then the other will withdraw, stonewall, or leave to avoid the discomfort. The first partner will then pursue more, driving the second partner deeper into withdrawal. Obviously, this will only lead to frustration by all. The only way out is to recognize what's going on and talk about it together. Name it, claim it, and change.

Draw Boundaries That Won't Set You Up.

When your partner asks something of you, be honest about your limitations. Going along with things that you don't truly want sets you up to feel disappointed and resentment later. You are responsible when you do that to yourself. Your partner cannot read your mind. Be honest and set boundaries that will serve everyone in the long run.

Respect Yourself & Express Your Thoughts/Feelings Openly.

You have the right to say what you think and feel. A relationship built on false information intended to please your partner will eventually fall apart. Strong relationships are built on trust and respect, which can only happen when both partners are honest with each other.

Beware of Keeping Secrets to Protect Your Partner.

We are often tempted to protect our partners by keeping secrets from them. This positive intention often falls apart as time passes and unexpected consequences come to light. It can be very difficult to know when to share "secrets." As much as you can, try to be as open as possible.

Take Responsibility for Your Own Limiting Beliefs.

We all have limiting beliefs. They are the small voices that whisper in the dark, trying to protect us, but keeping us stuck in fear. "I'll always be disappointed." "Men can't be trusted." "Women will only use you for your money." Your limiting beliefs are not your partner's fault. You had those beliefs long before your partner came along. Learn to identify your limiting beliefs. Be careful that you are not projecting your beliefs onto your partner.

Be True to Your Word.

Trust will be weak in struggling relationships. When you say you will do something or share what's true for you, your partner is going to trust that is true. It's ok for you to change your mind, but take the time to catch your partner up to speed. This allows your partner to grow and change with you.

Take the Time to Express Appreciation.

We often take it for granted that our partners will know we are grateful for them. When we don't take the time to express these simple appreciations, we begin to feel taken for granted. Thank your partner whenever he/she does things that make your life easier and better.

Daydream Together.

We enter relationships to build lives together. We often get caught up in the grind of life's logistics. Take the time to daydream together and explore what possibilities you both hope for in the future. Make goals and plans to support each other to live out your dreams.

HOW TO AVOID COMMUNICATION
THROUGH CONFLICTS

A conflict in a relationship may be defined as any kind of disagreement, including an argument, or an ongoing series of disagreements, for example, about how to spend money. Conflict can be extremely stressful, but it can also act to 'clear the air', surfacing issues that need discussion.

Conflicts and disagreements may result in us becoming angry, and they may also arise because we have become angry about something else. At work, we might try to control our anger and avoid saying things we might regret. At home, unfortunately, we are much more likely to say hurtful things to others as a result. There are also less likely to be others around who can mediate, and disagreements therefore quickly escalate in a way that might not happen at work.

This means that conflict in a relationship can rapidly become very unpleasant, and also very personal.

Sadly, when we are close to people, we often know how best to hurt them. In anger, that may be exactly what we want to do, however much we regret it later.

However, many people never get further than denial, smoothing over or fighting. The problem with this, however, is that these are not long-term strategies to resolve the issue. They are, at best, papering over the cracks, and this is not possible in a long-term relationship (or rather, the relationship is unlikely to prove long-term if this is your chosen approach).

As a general rule, honest communication about feelings, especially feelings about something being wrong, is always going to work better in a romantic relationship.

The key in a relationship, therefore, is to move beyond those three to compromise or, best of all, collaboration.

In a compromise, both of you give up something in favor of an agreed mid-point solution

This is likely to result in a better result than win/lose, but it's not quite a win/win. Because both of you have given something up, neither of you is likely to be completely happy with the outcome, which may lead to revisiting the discussion over and over again.

When you collaborate, by contrast, you work together to create a win/win situation, building on the conflict.

It does take time but, in a relationship, it is worth the investment.

Moving towards collaboration

The big question, of course, is how you can move towards collaboration, especially if you have already established a pattern of fighting. There are a few ideas that will help:

Talk before you are angry and agree a strategy

Managing conflict requires a commitment from both of you. Talk beforehand about how you would like to manage disagreements, and also agree that you will help each other to do that.

You may find it helpful to talk about how you behave when you are angry, and support each other to manage that. For example, if one of you becomes angry very quickly, it may be helpful for the other to propose waiting until later to talk.

Walk away when you are angry

Get into a habit of not discussing issues when you are angry. Say something like:

"I can't talk now, I'm just too angry. Please let's talk about this later when I've calmed down."

Then walk away, and go off somewhere to calm down.

Don't try to discuss difficult things when you are tired and/or hungry

We are all more likely to be grumpy and difficult when we are tired or hungry. It is human nature. Avoid having difficult conversations at difficult times. Instead, find a time when you are both relaxed and comfortable, and the conversations are less likely to escalate into an argument. Some people prefer to go out for a walk, and others find time at home is better: try things out and see what works best for you.

Always be prepared to apologize

You may feel that you were in the right. You may even have been in the right.

Being prepared to apologize for the way that your partner feels, however, will go a long way towards ensuring that they feel they have been heard, and that you understand their concerns. This is especially true if, despite your best intentions, you ended up shouting at each other.

Apologizing doesn't mean you have to accept that you were wrong.

It means saying that you are sorry that there was a disagreement, and you are sorry that your partner is upset, and that you are committed to finding a way forward that works for you both.

Listen and discuss

Be prepared to listen to your partner. Don't just repeatedly explain your own point of view or you will end up fighting again. Building a compromise or a collaborative solution requires real understanding of what is important to them, and why, and a discussion that shares viewpoints and opinions constructively.

MAIN CAUSES OF CONFLICT IN YOUR RELATIONSHIP

Relationships are made up of two people with different values and often different personalities.

These two people can provoke conflict when not fully aware or accepting of their differences. When I say "conflict", I mean disagreements or different points of view. However, it all comes down to behaviors and not knowing how to manage in certain situations.

Conflict is not a bad thing, as long as you are committed to the relationship and willing to work to fix it. Many times conflict can be a blessing. Why? Well, if your relationship is going perfectly fine that means someone is not being transparent. You both have the right to view things differently and to express it without hurting the other one. When conflict arises, both partners are usually being honest and voicing their opinion. However, what needs to be worked on is finding common ground.

Conflicts in relationships begin for many reasons. Before you try to fix a conflict you need to find the root cause of it. Many times people focus on the surface of the problem not the cause of it. This may for a while numb the symptoms (avoid the fights), but eventually, the problem will continue. For your own peace of mind, please be aware that all relationships have disagreements. Conflict does not mean your relationship is a failure. Also, conflict does not mean you can't be happy. Healthy relationships grow and mature through conflict.

The Five Main Causes of Conflict

1. Selfishness

Too often, we are so determined to get that "thing" we need, that we forget our decisions affect others. This is true for any type of relationship. Couples often have the conflict due to the fact that someone in the relationship fails to think of the other person when making decisions. Sometimes this is done knowingly and happens often, extending the life of the conflict. Selfishness is number one on the list because when a person cannot respect the needs of others, it becomes impossible to have a healthy relationship.

Don't be selfish; don't try to impress others. Be humble, thinking of others as better than yourselves.

2. Communication

"It is not what you say, but how you say it"

Communication is the method of getting it out there. Too often communicating in the relationship means argument, this causes tension and as a result, communication is avoided completely. Communicating the wrong way can cause further conflict in the relationship.

3. Resentment

There may be an occasion (or many) where one of the partners offends the other. When that individual fails to communicate the hurt the offense caused, he/she will keep those negative emotions in their heart causing resentment. This is where the root cause of conflict needs to be evaluated. At times the person will seem discontent or upset and will not say why. The person can also become distant, causing the other individual to think that they are not interested in the relationship.

4. Finger Pointing or Criticism

The most annoying thing is to be surrounded by a person who criticizes everything you do. The second most annoying thing is being surrounded by someone who claims that everything is your fault. Sometimes in relationships, this is the case. One partner accuses the other about everything that goes wrong or finds that he/she has a better way of doing things. The funny part of this is that when things do go right, that person claims responsibility right away.

5. Unrealistic or Distorted Expectations

This was a big one for me. You all have heard of "Prince Charming", "Happily Ever After" and so on. Well, sorry to burst your bubble, but it is not real. I grew up watching romantic movies and fairy tales that told me that somewhere existed a perfect man for me and that I would be happy. I thought there was nothing I need to do but wait for such great man. After kissing a few frogs, I realized there seemed to be an extinction of such men. Life experiences taught me that you have to build the life and happiness you want. Yes, a loving and accepting person at your side helps a lot, but you can't force that person to make you happy. Happiness is your responsibility. Many relationships have conflicts because one or both individuals feel that their expectations are not being met. Often, these expectations are unrealistic or distorted and the person will need a wake-up call back to reality.

STRATEGIES TO RESOLVE CONFLICT

1. Do not use any of the 4 horsemen

If you find yourself being defensive, or using criticism, stonewalling or contempt you will escalate the conflict AND significantly damage your relationship.

Instead of criticism, use a gentler way of explaining what is causing your problem

Avoid defensiveness by taking responsibility for what is your responsibility

Do not use contempt instead share your own feelings and needs

Instead of stonewalling, find ways to self sooth so that you can remain present

2. Getting to the problem

Describe to your partner what you feel the problem is. Be as specific as you can and then give them a chance to respond to what you have said. Keep an open mind. You're looking for a win/win so try to remain objective and keep the heat down.

3. Same fight just a different day

When you are fighting about the same issues over and over it is usually because there is a difference in core values and beliefs. These are attitudes that may have begun in childhood. Ask each other what the issues really mean and when did they first experience them. This can go a long way to you both understanding the issue rather than resolving it. Some issues cannot be resolved but with a better understanding they can be avoided or be less upsetting.

4. Shutdowns

The silent treatment can feel controlling, involves avoidance and can disempower your partner. If your partner is shutting you out let them know how it makes you feel and ask them to explain why they are upset. Ask them what they need from you. If this is a regular pattern in the relationship seek outside help from a therapist.

5. Deal Breakers

It is really important to avoid putting the relationship on the line when conflict happens. It can create anxiety about abandonment and makes it more difficult to resolve issues. It also erodes trust in the relationship. Don't threaten to leave the relationship unless you are actually considering it.

6. Don't sweat the small stuff

And a lot of it is small stuff. Ask yourself will this still bother me in a week or month's time? More often than not it won't. During any relationship there will be plenty of issues that arise so pick your fights.

7. Share the power and time

When you are having conflict remember to make space for your partner. Speak a little less and listen more. If you spend your time interrupting it will shut down the communication and can leave your partner feeling resentful.

8. Don't put pebbles in your pocket

Deal with issues as they arise. Don't hang on to small issues and then raise them all when conflict finally arises. Trying to deal with one topic at a time will mean that you are more likely to resolve the issue.

How to avoid a fight

If you want to prevent a fight from beginning, which is a good idea some of the time, like when you are getting ready to leave for work or you are really tired and need some sleep, then here are some great tips ...

Just listen if you are able – active listening helps your partner feel heard and may just be enough to help them work out for themselves the issue that is troubling them

Try to put yourself in their shoes – maybe they are raising a relevant point

Do NOT react! Take some long slow deep breaths and wait before you say anything – stopping even for a short time can help you calm down and give a gentler response

Stay clear of the four horsemen – they will escalate a conversation pretty quickly

Acknowledge your partners issue then suggest discussing it a little later in the day so that you can both have a think about the subject first

Use technology – email or text some of the issues. This can take any heated emotion out of the equation and allows you to be very specific when you are raising issues

What can you do if conflict is escalating?

Take a time out. Negotiate this ahead of time. If either party feels things are escalating then it is okay for the discussions to end. Let the other person know when you are willing to begin discussing the issue again. 30 minutes should calm the situation down.

If either party is becoming angry or using any of the four horsemen it is time to stop. Go do another activity or deal with the strong emotion that is happening. Try hitting a punch bag, going for a run, using some breathing exercises or being mindful.

Let the other partner know that you care about them and how they are feeling and that, despite the disagreement, you still love them.

If your partner attempts to repair things please be kind to them and consider accepting their attempt

How to repair

Following an argument it's really important to repair the relationship and reconnect with your partner. This requires both partners to sooth and support each other. You can achieve this by apologizing, hugging one another or sharing a calming activity. Also you can ask your partner what they need from you at that moment.

Relationships can be challenging but you choose to be with your partner because you care about them. Remember that you don't want to avoid conflict in your relationship, just find ways to manage it.

If you are struggling with unresolved conflict and you have tried some of the strategies I have talked about it might be time to bring in a third party. I work with couples to identify core values and beliefs that may be contributing to conflict and use a solution-focused approach to get the relationship back on track.

Ways to Reduce Conflict in Your Relationship

Conflict is a sign your relationship needs to grow.

Conflict is not inherently bad (or good), and neither is anger. Conflict is a necessary part of any relationship, and can move a relationship out of a stagnant state. It's healthy when it helps people see their own strengths and weaknesses, and all couples experience conflict at one time or another.

But conflict is unhealthy when it's the prevailing state, defining the relationship with a chaotic, loud, and tense energy. A basic ground of peace is necessary for any relationship to thrive and endure.

1. Give up your need to be right

The need to win every argument, every point, indicates emotional immaturity. If you really care about someone you don't want him or her to feel patronized, belittled, or manipulated—which is what happens when you fight your partner to validate your ego at every possible opportunity. And if you and your partner are constantly butting heads, and you didn't use to, it's a sign of deeper trouble in the relationship.

Relationships thrive when both people decide to bravely work through conflict together rather than retreat into battle positions and fight until the actual problem is forgotten and exhaustion sets in. Even if you know you're right, about whatever seems so important in that moment, is proving it worth making the most important person in your life feel stupid?

2. Don't use passive aggressive silent treatment

Not speaking to your partner when you're angry with him or her is a no-win communication strategy, but many people do it. It builds resentment between you and your partner and prolongs an argument. Despite leaps forward with Artificial Intelligence, we still can't read each other's minds, so glaring at your significant other and expecting them to know why you're so angry is not going to work. It will just make them feel punished, confused, or even angrier than you are.

To resolve a strong conflict, you have to have some faith in the other person—if you tell them honestly what's bothering you, will they listen or close you out? Set rules to fight fair, early in the relationship: no silent treatment, listen without judging, don't go to bed angry.

3. Choose your words

Your words start as thoughts, then turn into actions (which turn into habits, and character). When you constantly tear down your partner with mean words, patronizing tones, or ugly curses, you're building your character, and it's not pretty. Choose the words you speak with care, and pause to breathe in the middle of an argument. Besides dampening the potential in a relationship, constantly shooting out negative words like arrows will make your own life less interesting, less happy. Choosing words out of love and respect actually builds good karma, and it builds up the relationship. You'll hear more kind words in return, too.

4. Slow down your discussion

One of the strategies I'm often getting couples to do in my therapy room is to slow down. When you're triggered and feeling frustrated and angry in a conflict, it's hard to keep track of what's being said because the discussion moves so quickly. Slow down the process so you can listen carefully to what your partner is saying without reacting quickly. Take time to reflect before you respond. Just this simple strategy can completely change the conversation and de-escalate the rising tensions.

5. Let go of your hang-ups, let go of the past

Holding onto past hurts—from conflicts, perceived slights, a bad night's sleep, anything—increases their power over you. Don't keep a tally of who wins what argument in the relationship; it's juvenile and pointless. Forgiveness is giving up the hope of a better past. Bring your attention to this moment, to where the relationship is right now, free from the baggage of your last fight. That's the only way to move the relationship forward with dignity and new energy.

6. Repair quickly to get back on track

After a fight, whether it's mild or a category 5 cyclone, work to repair your relationship quickly. This includes making a sincere apology, if you need to take responsibility for causing your partner hurt. Maybe you and your partner couldn't resolve the conflict before you went to sleep, and you slept in separate beds because of this. First thing in the morning, sit down and talk. Don't go off to work still mad at each other. Lingering discord will affect both your days and the relationship will have one wheel off the track. Forgiveness gets easier every time you do it. The best couples seek to resolve hurts and conflict quickly, so they can get back on track and feel united.

7. Take care of your self

You can't care for a relationship properly if you're not caring for yourself too. Sleeping well, exercising, spending time breathing deeply in a quiet room: all of these acts of self-care will build up your physical and emotional health. They clear your head and lower your blood pressure. And they calm wild emotions, as from conflict in your relationship.

Tips for Resolving Conflict

Recognize that people come into our lives for a reason and even negative experiences are opportunities for growth. Be grateful for the learning experience, work towards acceptance, forgive and let go of the past. Consciously choose how you want to move forward.

"Whenever you're in conflict with someone, there is one factor that can make the difference between damaging your relationship and deepening it. That factor is attitude."

Conflict is a normal and natural aspect of relationships. As human beings, we are primed to respond to stress with a "fight" or "flee" response. Often, neither of these choices is appropriate. Therefore, we need to find a way to address conflict that is direct and assertive, while also respectful and diplomatic. Some people fear conflict and go to great lengths to avoid it, which can backfire and lead to emotional, relational and medical problems. If handled effectively, conflict can be an opportunity for learning, growth and positive change.

1. Pause and get grounded.

If your feathers are ruffled, it's best to take a moment to regroup before having a knee-jerk reaction you might regret later. Breathe deeply (in through your nose, down to your stomach and out through your mouth) to calm yourself. Check in with your body and recognize if there are any physical discomforts that are exacerbating your emotional agitation (i.e., hunger, fatigue, etc.).

If possible and appropriate, address those needs --
otherwise, raise a mental red flag so you are conscious
that your emotions may be inflamed by these
conditions. Stretching is a good way to quickly release
tension and achieve physical comfort and neutral
posture.

2. Zoom out to gain perspective.

Imagine you are viewing the conflict from a neutral
place at a greater distance. Imagine emotionally
unplugging or detaching from the situation to
increase awareness. Are you really upset about the
issue at hand or are you displacing your anger? For
example, are you flipping off the driver behind you
when you are actually mad at your boss about the
meeting you just left?

Make sure you address the appropriate person.
Identify the real issue and don't argue about the
minutia if there is a deeper core issue that needs to be
addressed. For example, don't argue about the toilet
seat being left up if you are actually mad that you are
feeling lonely or unsupported. Choose your battles: let
the little stuff go and care about yourself enough to
address the important matters.

3. Become mindful of your nonverbal communication.

Because much of communication is nonverbal, be aware of your facial expressions, hand gestures, and body language to ensure you are sending the message that you want to be received.

4. Avoid behaviors that add fuel to the fire.

Physical or verbal abuse is never acceptable.

5. Reflect empathy.

The ability to show you understand how the other person feels is perhaps the single most powerful communication skill. It allows the person to feel heard and diffuses conflict. You do not have to agree with their perspective, but you can show you understand their feelings (i.e., "I can understand that you felt upset by that.").

6. Take responsibility for yourself.

Save everybody time by owning up to your own poor behaviors. This is not a sign of weakness, rather it demonstrates awareness and integrity and will likely expedite successful resolution. Make sincere and timely amends and apologies.

7. Use assertive communication.

Avoid being passive (weak in setting boundaries); aggressive (hostile or entitled); or passive-aggressive (acting out through indirect behaviors like slamming a door or not responding to an email). Stay in the present and don't dredge up old issues from the past. Ask for what you need, say no to what you can't do, and be open to negotiation and compromise. Articulate a complaint about a specific behavior and express your feelings in a way that is clear, direct and appropriate.

Whenever possible, communicate directly in-person or over the phone versus email or text battles where misunderstandings breed quickly. Use "I" statements rather than "you" statements to reduce defensiveness. For example, "I am upset that I did not get the promotion," rather than "You are a jackass."

8. Be open and flexible.

Listen and really hear the other person. Ask questions to gather information that will be clarifying. Consider other perspectives or solutions. Look for the compromise or "win-win."

9. Focus on what you can control and let go of the rest.

"How people treat you is their karma; how you react is yours." You can control your own behaviors and responses but you cannot control others or the outcome. You can advocate for yourself in the context of a relationship and if resolution cannot be achieved, you can empower yourself to change the boundaries of that relationship or perhaps even end it altogether.

10. Forgive.

"Resentment is like drinking poison and then hoping it will kill your enemies." Recognize that people come into our lives for a reason and even negative experiences are opportunities for growth. Be grateful for the learning experience, work towards acceptance, forgive and let go of the past. Consciously choose how you want to move forward.

REASONS WE FAIL TO COMMUNICATE AND RESOLVE CONFLICT WELL

When we think about getting married, many fun and exciting things come to mind – the proposal, the ring, picking out the dress, the venue, the bridal party, etc. While those things definitely are enjoyable, there are also other types of preparation that need to be done as well – things that may not be as fun and exciting, but actually are much more important for the long haul. We need to prepare ourselves to develop a healthy relationship, acquiring the relationship skills needed to have a healthy marriage.

Many of us are not very proficient in these relationship skills. Perhaps they have never been modeled for us, or we have not been exposed to them much. Some of us are not naturally gifted in these areas. While that may be true, it does not mean that we are permanently at a disadvantage. These relationship skills can be learned, just like riding a bike! With practice and repetition, we can become proficient in their use.

The two most important skills necessary to create a successful, enriching marriage are communication and conflict resolution. These skills are interrelated and interconnected with each other. Communication is connecting with another person through the sharing of feelings, thoughts, wants and needs. It is the process by which we invite another person into our world and our experience; it is how we are known. Conflict resolution utilizes communication in order to help resolve the inevitable misunderstandings and disruptions in our connections with others so that our relationships can deepen and can be more securely, emotionally connected.

Why We Fail to Communicate/Resolve Conflict

1. "I don't know how to communicate or resolve conflict."

Oftentimes, we just don't know how to open up and/or express ourselves. Communicating and resolving conflict were not done well in our families growing up. Because these skills were never modeled for us, we don't have any idea of how to do them. We may be capable of using these skills, but we do not know how to get started or what it looks like to put them into practice.

2. "I don't even know what I am feeling."

Related to not knowing how is that we may not even know what we are feeling. If communicating and resolving conflict were never done in our families growing up, then we may never have developed an awareness of our feelings because we never really paid any attention to them. Maybe we were discouraged from feeling or expressing them, or maybe we were even punished for doing so. Growing up did you ever hear the expression "Stop crying or I'll give you something to cry about!"? Children are not really encouraged to explore, experience, or express their feelings when they hear that.

This can also occur if we have an avoidant attachment style, where we avoid our feelings, or we avoid experiencing them, because they are just too uncomfortable. Because of that, we suppress them, push them down, stuff them, ignore them, and we can shut down emotionally. With enough time and practice doing this, we eventually don't even know what our feelings are anymore – we just have no idea what we are feeling.

3. "It's just too scary to share!"

Sometimes we don't want to share or talk about conflict because it is just too scary to open up and be vulnerable. We might think we will be seen as weak if we do, or maybe we think that others will take advantage of us if we express our feelings.

When we haven't learned how to handle strong emotions, especially those that may come up during a conflict, we may feel overwhelmed or scared by strong emotions. So, we shut them down, close them off, or ignore them. Or, if we have little practice managing strong emotions and stuff them instead, we may fear losing control. We may have a sense that those feelings are there, buried, and we fear that if we let them come out, they are going to explode and take over. We may fear that we will get lost in them and that the ensuing chaos will never end. Clients have described these overwhelming feelings as continuously pounding ocean waves that never stop.

4. "I shouldn't share my feelings – I don't want to offend or make the situation worse!"

Sometimes we are afraid that if we do share what we think or feel, especially during a conflict, we will actually make the situation worse. We surely don't want to cause more problems, and so we don't say anything, or we just disregard our feelings.

We also may fear offending the other person. So, we would rather just ignore our feelings than risk offending someone else. We figure that we can just absorb it and it will be ok – "it's just my issue." We don't want to rock the boat, and so we take the path of lowest risk.

5. "I'm not worthy of being heard, or I don't deserve to be heard."

Sometimes we don't feel entitled to what we are feeling, and so we don't express it. We might think that our spouses' thoughts or feelings are more important than ours because of our low self-esteem, and so we do not share ours. We might feel, "I'm not as important as you are, and so I do not think that my thoughts should be listened to by you."

For example, you might have had a horrible day at work, but when you get home and begin to tell your spouse, she has something to share about her day. So, you clam up and do not share your own experiences and feelings, and you stuff them down again.

6. "My feelings are/can be sinful!"

In some Christian circles or homes, strong feelings, especially anger, are seen as sinful. Sometimes the expression of feelings can be seen as selfish or manipulative. As a result, their expression may be discouraged, muffled, shut down, or worse, punished. This happens especially when parents or leaders themselves are not comfortable with their own feelings or their expression. Because they are not comfortable with it, it is hard for them to allow any sort of healthy expression of their feelings or anyone else's.

7. We are sabotaging our efforts.

Sometimes we try to talk and express ourselves, but the way we attempt to communicate actually makes it harder for the other person to hear us or respond well to us. When we engage in these behaviors, we make it very difficult for the other person to hear us or respond well to us. We set ourselves up to not be heard or responded well to.

These are some various reasons why maybe we don't communicate and resolve conflict. Hopefully they are helpful in building some understanding of why it may be so difficult for us to communicate or resolve conflict well. It is often helpful to think through our family of origin concerning how thoughts and feelings were communicated and how conflicts were resolved in order to understand our present difficulties in communication.

Effective Communication for Resolving Conflict Successfully

Conflict can ignite from the smallest word or action and can spark destructive responses and behaviors. Unresolved or poorly navigated conflict can damage and even destroy relationships. However, conflict does not have to be destructive. Handled effectively, conflict can actually contribute to stronger, deeper relationships and can help to address ongoing problems and concerns. Effective communication skills serve a key role in successfully resolving conflict, both in the home and in the workplace.

Effective Communication Skills

An effective communication skill for successfully resolving conflicts is to address only one issue at a time and avoid introducing other topics, even if they are related. Clearly specify what you are concerned about, even if it takes some time to isolate the primary issue at hand. Also, avoid attacking the other person or making accusations, which will only lead to distrust and defensiveness. To listen effectively, take care to make sure you understand what the other person is trying to say, restating that person's thoughts and feelings as needed. Strong verbal and nonverbal communication involves making appropriate eye contact, not using threatening physical actions, and verbally expressing how the situation makes you feel, instead of attacking or accusing the other person.

There are many benefits that come from learning to resolve conflicts through effective communication. One notable benefit of using effective communication to resolve conflict is a reduction in anxiety, whether within a family or in the workplace. "Conflict has an emotional cost that remains after the battle is over," and unresolved conflict ultimately impedes "satisfying, functional relationships." Successfully resolving conflict also brings about greater trust and intimacy in relationships. Learning effective communication skills can help you to avoid the ongoing stress and discomfort that often results from unresolved conflict.

CONCLUSION

Communication is vitally important for sports teams, government, education, business and most all important human endeavors, including personal relationships and marriage. Without communications, seemingly insignificant situations can turn into major problems that scare emotions deeply. Communication in a marriage or relationship may sound like an obvious thing, and something of extreme importance from a common sense standpoint. But when things go wrong, emotion can take over and throw common sense out the window.

Communication in any interpersonal relationship is paramount, whether it is job related, relatives, long-term friends or intimate. Those who fail to understand the importance of relationship communication are sure to fail over and over again in their most important relationships. Failure to communicate can cause a catastrophe for couples, thus ground rules or an understanding should be set forth early on. Open communication can help blossom a relationship to greater heights and more meaningful dialogue at a personal level.

Relationship Communication is very important in sustaining a marriage. Communication problems in relationship are often the primary issue of failed marriages. So, to make sure that your marriage doesn't fail because of communication, you need to learn to develop good communication skills in your relationship.

Relationship communication can be tricky. It is a curious way to start an article but consider this. Relationships involve people.

You are a unique human being. The people that you are in relationships with are also human beings and also unique. Every one of you has been brought up in a unique environment known as a family that is composed of other unique individuals.

We come into this world in a manner that is somewhat random. By random, we have little choice about the human beings who will be guiding us towards becoming adults. We do not know what beliefs they may have and we do not know if those beliefs and the resulting actions will be effective in dealing with the world out there. Worse still, we have no idea whatsoever about how well what we are being taught will enable us to cope with other human beings.

Given the apparent randomness of human upbringing, it is a miracle that we are not rushing to push "the button" every 5 min. So what is it that binds us together as a species? What is it that brings you together with another person in a relationship?

A lot depends on what you focus on. It is rumored that leaving the top off of the toothpaste tube is one of the leading causes of divorce. This is of course complete fabrication. The leading cause of problems in relationship communication is bad focus.

Good communication comes from focusing on the things that work for both of you and for the relationship. By switching your focus from the top on the toothpaste tube, to appreciative remarks, and by focusing on the good things, your perspective changes.

Many people are quite concerned with allowing certain information about themselves to get out, but keeping secrets from your closest friends or lovers can cause challenges later on. It therefore, behooves you to pick your friends and partners carefully, if you do not trust your partner or friend, you might have to ask why they are your friends in the first place. Once you have chosen to have a special relationship, you must understand that you have to communicate and that old cliché; "the truth, the whole truth and nothing but the truth" ought to ring through.

Of course, with any relationship, communication is a two-way street, it is okay to give, but without reciprocation, you will find even greater problems down the road. The secret to success in relationships is communication, without it, you have nothing but pretend friends.

Frequently, couples request suggestions for how to boost their intimacy, better their communication skills, increase passion in their sexual relationship, etc. The following are 10 suggestions to relationship building, which incorporate communication, sex, and individual responsibility. It should be understood that exercises in couple's therapy could be extremely beneficial and useful; however, depending on troubles the couple may be experiencing these exercises may only provide a Band-Aid placed on a much bigger wound. Couples therapy can serve as a tool to practice and utilize the exercise while exploring how these patterns and interactions were started.

Setting a time once a month to commit to speaking to your partner about your relationship. This dialogue should include your likes and dislikes about the relationship. This exercise is designed to allow partners to express their feelings rather than allowing resentment to build over time. This could simply be 15 minutes at the end of the day when you and your partner can commit to not be disturbed by other things and communicate with each other.

The ability to speak to your partner in a way that allows you to be heard and also without provoking defenses is a difficult balance to achieve. Learning how to communicate better should include the ability to also listen. First you must learn how to both listen and speak out of your thoughts and feelings rather than from your defenses. Were our parents' right when they told us to "turn the other cheek"? Walking away until you are able to listen and speak calmly allows you to be more attentive to your partner when you are communicating.

During communication, try using "I" statements, such as "I feel angry when you come home late at night" rather than "you make me angry when you come home late at night". This allows for you to express your feelings without also expressing blame to your partner. Communication tends to run more smoothly this way, rather than you and your partner becoming defensive when you are trying to communicate your needs.

Thinking of things that are important in our life and giving priority to particular aspects can be quite important. When we put our relationship aside this sends a strong message to our partner, which we may not be trying to send; however, the message is we are not willing to give our time and effort to a committed relationship.

Isn't it interesting that during the dating phase, our relationship meant everything? We gave this our utmost attention and put all priorities aside to make room for our new attraction. How is it that we made time then to put everything aside, but we cannot now? Do we get set in our ways or do we fear being vulnerable and compromising? Relationships are not easy; they require work and attention that people need to be ready for.

The idea of being attentive is awareness to what is happening in your relationship. Many times, partners attempt to "brush problems under the rug" and ignore the obvious. This only builds resentments and hurt feelings in the relationship. People should address problems as they come rather than hiding behind them to allow them to accumulate.

The healthy balance between being passive and being aggressive is assertiveness. Being assertive with your partner allows you to state your needs and wants in a direct and reasonable way. This also allows you to express thoughts, opinions, feelings and ideas without holding them inside and wishing later you would have said them. You can convey your thoughts in a way that expresses what you want; however, not instructing or ordering someone as in an aggressive communication style. Finding the balance of assertiveness is difficult, but worth the time to practice.

Soothing our own feelings without reacting from intense emotions allows us to appropriately communicate. During times of intense emotions, we tend to react with this same level of emotion rather than soothing ourselves and calming ourselves down. The ability to comfort yourself also means you must calm yourself even when your feelings are hurt and your partner is not validating you or telling you what you want to hear.

Resolving a conflict can seem overwhelming because we sometimes allow conflicts to continue and hurt feelings begin to emerge. Not allowing conflict to go unresolved or resentment to build is essential for couples. Conflict resolution should take place when you and your partner are calm and willing to talk until you can reach a compromise. Resolving a conflict involves coming into the talk with things you want to change and an agreement that you are willing to change the things that you can.

Your sexual relationship can at times, be a metaphor for how you are functioning as a couple. It is important that you are open and honest with your partner about your sexual relationship and to be open and honest with yourself. First, if you do not already know yourself, your own body, and your own likes and dislikes then take time to be alone, comfortable, and uninterrupted to sit in your bedroom, bathroom, shower or other comfortable place to explore your body and find out what touch you like. This will allow you to be more confident and calm when you are with your partner and increase the likelihood that you will share your likes and dislikes with him or her as well.

Initially, try exploring each other's bodies with touch from hands or lips, without focus on the genitals or penetration and verbally share the things that feel good with each other. Try this for several days while later focusing on the genitals and again share what things you enjoy most with your partner.

Looking within ourselves and searching how we contribute to the problems in the relationship is something most people stray from. This activity can be very difficult and most people tend to look for blame in their partner and not within themselves. First, think of the common arguments you and your partner have and explore how you contribute to these disagreements. Most of the time we seek to change our partner rather than change ourselves.

Maintaining a balance between your identity as an individual and your identity as a couple can be very difficult. Having this balance is extremely important for the relationship; however, because we tend to appreciate our relationship much more when we have our own independence and autonomy, it is a crucial aspect to all of our relationships.

9 781678 061326